THE RULE OF GOD

Colin Dye

Sovereign World

Sovereign World Ltd
PO Box 777
Tonbridge
Kent TN11 0ZS
England

Scriptural quotations are from the New King James Version,
Thomas Nelson Inc., 1991.

ISBN: 1 85240 202 4

Typeset by CRB Associates, Reepham, Norfolk
Printed and bound by Interpak Books, Pietermaritzburg

FOREWORD

The material in this *Sword of the Spirit* series has been developed over the past ten years at Kensington Temple in London as we have sought to train leaders for the hundreds of churches and groups we have established. Much of the material was initially prepared for the students who attend the International Bible Institute of London – which is based at our church.

Over the years, other churches and colleges have asked if they may use some of our material to help them establish training courses for leaders in their towns and countries. This series has been put together partly to meet this growing need, as churches everywhere seek to train large numbers of new leaders to serve the growth that God is giving.

The material has been constantly refined – by myself, by the students as they have responded, by my many associate pastors, and by the staff at the Bible Institute. In particular, my colleague Timothy Pain has been responsible for sharpening, developing and shaping my different courses and notes into this coherent series.

I hope that many people will use this series in association with our developing Satellite Bible School, but I also pray that churches around the world will use the books to train leaders.

We live at a time when increasing numbers of new churches are being started, and I am sure that we will see even more startling growth in the next few decades. It is vital that we re-examine the way we train and release leaders so that these new churches have the best possible biblical foundation. This series is our contribution to equipping tomorrow's leaders with the eternal truths that they need.

Colin Dye

CONTENTS

INTRODUCTION

It is absolutely crucial that you get the title of this book in the *Sword of the Spirit* series right. It is 'The Rule of God' not 'The Rules of God' – that little letter 's' makes a huge difference!

The period of time from the giving of 'the Law' to Moses on Mount Sinai until the coming of Christ was the age of 'The Rules of God'. In that age, because of their sin and disobedience, God's children could not know God intimately and personally. So priests acted as mediators between the people and God, prophets passed on God's word, judges and kings governed the people, and 'the Law' ruled over them all.

People who loved God, and wanted to please him, had to keep all his rules – the totality of the regulations given through Moses and recorded in Exodus, Leviticus and Deuteronomy. Only through keeping *all* these rules, could people know God and be accepted by him.

But the age of 'The Rules of God' ended with the coming in Christ of 'The Kingdom of God'. Because of Christ's perfect obedience and sacrificial death, all people can now know God intimately and personally. The Great High Priest has, once-and-for-all, acted as mediator so that we all can approach God ourselves. The Great Prophet has come as God's incarnate Word so that we can know exactly what God is like, can know him for ourselves, and can hear him speaking personally to each one of us. The Judge of the whole earth, the King of kings, personally governs his people with grace and mercy. He himself rules supreme over all people who submit to his authority.

We will see that the New Testament makes it clear that the coming of Christ has set us free from 'the Law'. We are now called to be ruled by our gracious, merciful God rather than by a collection of rules.

How sad it is, therefore, when some Christian leaders try to lead God's people back into legalism, to urge believers to live by God's Old Testament rules (or rather, to keep a tiny selection of them), and to keep on introducing human rules and regulations into the church.

This book is essentially for those believers who will set aside their own ideas about God's kingdom, and will study God's word for themselves to discover God's revelation for living. Please make sure that you read each scriptural reference – ticking the boxes in the margin as you go along. Please answer every question and think through each point as it is made. Before moving on to a new section, always think carefully about the implications of what you have studied for your situation. Please allow God to speak to you as you study his word.

At the end of the book, there is some activity material. Please make sure that you study Parts 1–9 before starting to work through the activities. This will ensure that you have an overview of the biblical principles about God's rule before you try to apply the details of any one aspect. The activities will help you to grasp and apply the material you have studied.

You will also be able to use the activity pages when you teach the material to small groups. Please feel free to photocopy these pages and distribute them to any group you are leading. Although you should work through all the activities when you are studying on your own, please don't expect a small group to cover all the activity material. Instead, prayerfully select those parts that you think are most relevant for your group. This means that, at some meetings you might use all the material, whilst at others you might use only a small part.

It is my prayer that, through studying this book, you will see God's kingdom more clearly, will enter into his kingdom more deeply, and will consciously submit to him and be directed by him in every area of your life. I pray that you will live as one who has been liberated from rules and released into the personal rule and reign of the King of kings.

Colin Dye

PART ONE

the kingdom

The kingdom of God – or the kingdom of heaven – is the main theme of Jesus. He teaches far more about it than any other topic. Matthew's gospel – which is directed at a Jewish readership – calls it 'the kingdom of heaven', whereas Mark and Luke use 'the kingdom of God'.

Matthew almost certainly uses 'the kingdom of heaven' because Jews avoided using God's name and he did not want to offend his readers. But both expressions refer to the same reality – as can be seen by comparing Matthew 5:3 and Luke 6:20.

Matthew 5:3 ☐

Luke 6:20 ☐

WHAT IS THE KINGDOM?

The Greek word for kingdom, *basileia*, is derived from *basileus* – which means king. *Basileia* means sovereignty, royal power, dominion, kingly authority – the activity of ruling. It does not mean the country or people ruled by a king.

When we think about 'kingdom' in English today, we tend to mean a country or nation. But *basileia* means 'God's reign' rather than 'God's realm'. It describes an activity of God, rather than a nation or a place. It turns our attention away from ourselves and towards him.

In an attempt to reflect this important truth and avoid any misunderstanding, this book is called 'the Rule of God' rather than 'the Kingdom of God'.

This use of 'kingdom' as a ruling activity is seen in Old Testament passages like Psalm 22:28; 103:19; 145:8–13 & Daniel 4:25. They describe God's kingdom in terms which stress the gracious way that he rules.

The idea of a ruling activity is especially clear in the New Testament in Matthew 6:10 & Luke 11:2 – where the coming of the kingdom is linked with the doing of God's will.

The Jewish background

In the Old Testament, God is often portrayed both as the king of Israel – for example, Exodus 15:18; Deuteronomy 33:5; Isaiah 43:15; and as the king of all men – Jeremiah 46:18. His kingdom or reign is referred to in Deuteronomy 4:3; 1 Chronicles 29:11 & Obadiah 1:21.

There is a sense in which God's kingdom or rule is both present and future in the Old Testament. God is presented as the present, ultimate ruler of men and women, but – in passages like Isaiah 24:23 – the prophets also looked forward to a time when it would be evident that God visibly ruled among his people.

By the time of Jesus, there was a widespread hope and expectation among Jews that God would decisively intervene, liberate them from their enemies and restore their fortunes. They believed that the Messiah – another David – would come and prepare the way for the visible kingdom or ruling of God among them.

Some Jews expected another leader who would be an even greater earthly ruler then King David. Others looked forward to a heavenly kingdom and the emergence of 'the Son of Man' as foretold in Daniel 7. Most people probably had no clear idea what the kingdom would be like: they simply hoped and believed that it would soon be present.

Psalm 22:28 ☐
103:19 ☐
145:8–13 ☐

Daniel 4:25 ☐

Matthew 6:10 ☐

Luke 11:2 ☐

Exodus 15:18 ☐

Deuteronomy 33:5 ☐

Isaiah 43:15 ☐

Jeremiah 46:18 ☐

Deuteronomy 4:3 ☐

1 Chronicles 29:11 ☐

Obadiah 1:21 ☐

Isaiah 24:23 ☐

Daniel 7 ☐

John's announcement

Matthew 3:2 records John the Baptist's first announcement that God's kingdom was close at hand. It is hard for us to realise how sensational this announcement would have been at that time. John's message would have had massive significance as the Jews expected that the coming of the kingdom of God would be the turning point of history. They were right. It was. But the kingdom did not take the form that they expected.

Matthew 3:2 ☐

The Jewish religious leaders were right to believe that the arrival of the kingdom meant God would no longer reign from a distance. But they failed to grasp this meant that he would not continue to rule through blanket rules – through the Law. Instead, God's coming in person to establish his kingdom meant that he now ruled personally – through the Son and the Spirit.

They were also correct in their belief that the kingdom would rout their enemy, but – sadly – they had mistaken their *real* enemy.

They were also right to believe that the kingdom would reach all round the earth. However, they were wrong to think that this would happen immediately or by force. In Christ, God had not come to impose his rule on all people, merely to rule those who would willingly accept his reign.

Matthew 3:1–12 and Luke 3:7–20 show how John the Baptist taught that the coming kingdom or rule of God would:

Matthew 3:1–12 ☐

Luke 3:7–20 ☐

- mean judgement, sifting and purification for all humanity

- bring a moral challenge which could not be ignored

- be connected with the activity of Jesus

- mean that people must repent and be baptised

THE PRESENT KINGDOM

Jesus began his ministry by announcing in Mark 1:14–15 that the time had come and the kingdom of God was at hand. This must mean that some great event was about to take place.

Mark 1:14–15 ☐

Matthew 12:28 ☐

Luke 11:20 ☐

In Matthew 12:28 and Luke 11:20, Jesus repeats his claim that the kingdom has come and evidences this by casting out demons. This authority over evil spirits shows both that the kingdom of heaven has broken into the rule of the evil one, and also that the true king rules more effectively.

Luke 10:1–20 ☐

When Jesus sent the 72 disciples out to preach, in Luke 10:1–20, they announced the arrival of the kingdom: as a result, 'Satan fell like lightning from heaven'. All Jesus' miraculous activity proves that the kingdom has come.

Matthew 11:2–5 ☐

Luke 7:18–23 ☐

When John the Baptist began to doubt whether Jesus was the One he had been sent to announce, he sent his disciples to search out the answer. Matthew 11:2–5 & Luke 7:18–23 describes what convinced them that Jesus was the One who was ushering in the kingdom.

Jesus not only promised miracles in the future and forgiveness at the day of judgement, he also offered them both in the present – through himself. The kingdom came in and with Jesus. As the long-expected Messiah, Jesus is central to everything the Gospels announce about the kingdom, and the kingdom is central to everything Jesus teaches.

Matthew 3:17 ☐

- He is introduced as the beloved Son of God at his baptism – Matthew 3:17.

Matthew 17:5 ☐

- He is announced as the beloved Son of God at his transfiguration – Matthew 17:5.

Matthew 3:16 ☐

- He is filled with God's Spirit – Matthew 3:16.

Matthew 21:27 ☐

- He is invested with full divine authority – Matthew 21:27.

Luke 4:21 ☐

Matthew 5:17 ☐

- The Scriptures are fulfilled or completed in his coming – Luke 4:21 Matthew 5:17.

Mark 1:38 ☐

- He came to announce the kingdom or rule of God – Mark 1:38.

Luke 19:10 ☐

- He came to seek and save the lost – Luke 19:10.

Mark 10:45 ☐

- He came to serve others and give his life as a ransom for many – Mark 10:45.

Matthew 7:23 ☐

Matthew 25:41 ☐

- The secret of belonging to the kingdom or rule of God lies in belonging to him – Matthew 7:23; 25:41.

In teaching that the kingdom had arrived, had come, had begun, was among people and was a present reality, Jesus also taught – in

Matthew 11:11–12; Luke 7:28 & 16:16 – that some violence was associated with the arrival of the kingdom.

This does not mean that the kingdom was being established by physical violence. Rather, Jesus was pointing out the hostility of the world to the kingdom. John had already suffered and been imprisoned, and Jesus was warning those who would accept his rule that they must expect hostility – not just in the future, but also in the present.

THE FUTURE KINGDOM

As well as teaching that the kingdom had come, Jesus also taught that the kingdom was 'not yet'. For example, in Matthew 5:1–10, many of the kingdom benefits are set in the future. Although 'the blessed' already possess the kingdom, there is something still to come in the future – comfort, inheritance, mercy and so on.

Jesus' prayer in Matthew 6:10 is also both present and future. If the kingdom had fully come, we would not need to pray for it to come.

In Matthew 7:21–22, Jesus refers to a future day of reckoning when he is speaking about entering the kingdom. It is much the same in Matthew 8:11 & Luke 13:28–29.

Throughout Jesus' ministry, he looked forward to a day when the kingdom would come. We can see this in Matthew 13:42–43; 16:27–28; 20:21; 26:29; Mark 9:1; 10:37; 14:25 & Luke 22:18.

As we study and examine God's rule, we must always keep these two elements in mind. The kingdom is both 'now' and 'not yet'. We can experience God's rule now but we also look forward to knowing it in the future. There is much for us now, but there is more still to come.

This means that we should work to establish God's kingdom now, yet we should work knowing that the kingdom will not be fully established until some future date.

Too many believers focus on either the present or the future. Some are pre-occupied with serving God on earth, yet lack the hope and joy which comes from looking to the coming kingdom. Others are so pre-occupied with 'the last day' that they do not establish the kingdom

Matthew
    11:11–12 ☐

Luke 7:28 ☐

Luke 16:16 ☐

Matthew 5:1–10 ☐

Matthew 6:10 ☐

Matthew 7:21–22 ☐

Matthew 8:11 ☐

Luke 13:28–29 ☐

Matthew
    13:42–43 ☐
    16:27–28 ☐
    20:21 ☐
    26:29 ☐

Mark 9:1 ☐
    10:37 ☐
    14:25 ☐

Luke 22:18 ☐

around them on earth. A true understanding and application of the kingdom embraces both the present and the future – as Christ did.

ASPECTS OF THE KINGDOM

If we are to understand the kingdom rightly, we must appreciate four principal aspects.

1.   It belongs to God

It is the kingdom *of God*. It is an ongoing sovereign activity of God. He is in charge. He alone rules. It is not democratic! It is not an invitation to good works or social action. God himself has acted in history and he demands the utmost self-denial of all men and women.

2.   It is dynamic and powerful

Nothing to do with God can be weak or ineffective. The kingdom is not a temporary experiment. It is the permanent coming of the all-powerful king to rule his people and rout his enemies. In Luke 11:20–22, Jesus describes the present existence of the kingdom in terms of overcoming the armed strong man. The powerful overthrowing of demonic forces is central to the kingdom.

Luke 11:20–22 ☐

3.   It is established by Jesus

In Luke 1:32–33, an angel introduces Jesus as the one who will occupy David's throne and whose kingdom will never end. In his announcement, John the Baptist also makes clear the link between Jesus and the kingdom of God.

Luke 1:32–33 ☐

Throughout the Gospels, the kingdom and the Son of Man are inseparably linked – for example, Matthew 16:28 & Mark 9:1. This means that Jesus the Messiah – the Christ, the Anointed One – is God's agent and acts on his behalf to establish the kingdom of God.

Matthew 16:28 ☐

Mark 9:1 ☐

4. It is for salvation

The coming of the kingdom shows God's kingly activity in reaching out to save and bless people of every nation and generation. The driving out of devils evidences the king's power; the healings demonstrate his compassion, but the forgiveness of sins is the most prominent miracle in the proclamation of the kingdom – Luke 5:20–21.

Luke 5:20–21 ☐

THE MYSTERY OF THE KINGDOM

Much of Jesus' teaching about the kingdom is given in the form of parables. Matthew 13:1–52; Mark 4:10–12 & Luke 8:9–10 show how Jesus used parables to reveal what had been concealed – but only to those who really wanted to learn the true meaning of the kingdom. His use of parables ensured that the kingdom would remain concealed to those who were not serious seekers.

Matthew 13:1–52 ☐

Mark 4:10–12 ☐

Luke 8:9–10 ☐

This means that only those people who are determined to understand and enter the kingdom – who have an open, responsive mental attitude – will understand Jesus' parables of the kingdom. Several themes seem to run through the parables.

Certain growth

Growth occurs in several parables of the kingdom recorded in Matthew 13 – for example, the Sower (1–23), the Tares (24–30) and the Mustard Seed (31–32).

Only one type of 'soil' in four may be productive, but that yields impressive results. It might be hard to identify the 'good seed' in the kingdom, but it keeps on growing through to God's harvest. There might be a tiny beginning, but amazing growth will certainly follow.

Hidden nature

The parable of the Leaven – or yeast – (33) shows that outstanding results are achieved by inconspicuous methods. This is exactly the opposite of worldly thinking and practice.

Great value

Matthew 13:1–52 ☐

The parables of the Treasure (44) and the Pearl (45–46) show the incomparable value of the kingdom – yet its value is not appreciated or sought by all.

Puzzling mixture

The Dragnet (47–52) and the Tares (24–30) show that the righteous and the unrighteous stay mixed up in the world until the end time. No attempt must be made to separate them before the end, because only the king can act as judge. He alone can be trusted to distinguish correctly and not damage one of the righteous by mistake.

International nature

Matthew
21:33–46 ☐

The parable of the Vineyard, in Matthew 21:33–46, implies that the kingdom is not only for the Jews but also for people of other nations.

Repentance and obedience

Matthew
21:28–32 ☐

The Two Sons, Matthew 21:28–32, shows the need for repentance and obedience. Even tax collectors and prostitutes will enter the kingdom before religious leaders – if they fulfil the conditions of entry and the leaders do not.

Strong warnings

Matthew 25:1–13 ☐
Matthew 22:1–14 ☐

The parables of the Virgins, Matthew 25:1–13, and the Marriage Feast, Matthew 22:1–14, are strong warnings against ignoring or treating lightly the call of the kingdom. Please note how, although the warning is set in the future, its challenge is in the present.

Great opposition

The thorns in the Sower and the enemy in the Tares show that the Kingdom is opposed at every turn. Although growth takes place, it is always resisted.

THE KINGDOM IN THE NEW TESTAMENT

We have noted that the kingdom is the dominant theme in Jesus' teaching: it is mostly recorded in Matthew, Mark and Luke – especially Matthew. In this book, we will examine much of Christ's teaching about the kingdom, but we will base our studies in the early part of Matthew which is commonly called 'The Sermon on the Mount'.

Matthew 5–7 contains Christ's clearest teaching about the kingdom – yet many people misunderstand these chapters by interpreting them as 'more rules from God' rather than descriptions of a life 'ruled by God'.

The terms 'the kingdom of heaven' and 'the kingdom of God' do not appear very often in the rest of the New Testament. However, the concepts of the active personal rule of God in Christ and freedom from the Mosaic rules of God run throughout the New Testament. Phrases like 'the Lordship of Christ' are used instead of 'the kingdom', but they merely express the same truth in different words.

However, the wider New Testament use of 'the kingdom' must be part of any understanding of God's present and future rule.

John's Gospel

- Jesus links seeing and entering the kingdom with regeneration in 3:1–21. The kingdom is the activity of God and nobody can see it or enter it without being born again/regenerated *by God*. It is all the work of God and not of human beings.   John 3:1–21 ☐

- Jesus speaks to Pilate about his kingdom in 18:33–38. He distinguishes between political and spiritual ideas of kingship, and shows that his ruling does not overwhelm – instead it testifies.   John 18:33–38 ☐

Acts

- In Acts 19:8; 20:25 & 28:23, 'the kingdom' is used to describe the content of preaching and testimony. Acts normally uses 'the word of the Lord' to sum up preaching – as in 19:10 – and these two phrases seem to mean the same thing. We can say both that God's word is his rule, and that he rules through his word.   Acts 19:8–10 ☐   20:25 ☐   28:23 ☐

- Similarly, 20:24–25 parallels the kingdom with 'the gospel of grace' and 28:23 & 28:31 link speaking about the kingdom with teaching about the Lord Jesus Christ.

Paul's letters

- Romans 14:17 corrects those who think the kingdom should be about rules and regulations.

- 1 Corinthians 4:20 shows that the kingdom is not a matter of talk.

- 1 Thessalonians 2:12 makes it plain that members of the kingdom – people living under the rule of God – are expected to live lives worthy of God.

- 1 Corinthians 6:9–10; Galatians 5:21 & Ephesians 5:5 imply a future inheritance of the kingdom – and this is the basis for an appeal for moral behaviour. Immorality and impurity exclude believers from receiving their inheritance.

- 1 Corinthians 15:50 reminds us that the kingdom is not entered through human effort.

- Colossians 4:11 assumes that the kingdom is the goal of Paul's missionary work.

- Colossians 1:13–14 links the kingdom with salvation and forgiveness, and suggests the same kind of dynamic overthrow of evil powers as the Gospels. It is expressed differently, but the concept is the same.

- 2 Thessalonians 1:5; 2 Timothy 4:1 & 4:18 place the kingdom in the future.

- 1 Corinthians 15:24–28 describes Christ handing the kingdom back to the Father – but the main thrust of the passage is that Christ is already reigning. It emphasises a present activity while at the same time pointing to a future climax.

Other letters

- Hebrews 12:28 suggests a present experience and a future hope.

- James 2:5 mentions inheritance.

- 2 Peter 1:11 describes entering the kingdom.

- Revelation contains several references to the kingdom, and nearly all of them describe the kingdom being opposed and the ultimate dawning of the kingdom – for example, 1:9; 11:15; 12:10. The vision of the New Jerusalem in Revelation is presented as the fulfilment of all the biblical promises about a future kingdom.

We can see that the same themes run through the kingdom passages – present and future, opposition, salvation, inheritance, the word and grace of God.

Acts 1:3 shows that Jesus taught the disciples about the kingdom during the forty day period between his resurrection and ascension.

It was one thing for the disciples to try and understand the personal rule of God when Jesus was present in person. But how would the kingdom, the rule of God, work when Jesus was no longer with them in person?

Presumably Jesus gave them instructions about how to live and what to preach, for Acts 17:7 shows they carried on proclaiming Jesus as king. The rule of God gripped the lives of the early Christians and characterised the revolutionary message they proclaimed. Jesus was their ruler – whether they expressed this in terms of a 'king', to Jews, or as 'the Lord' (the Caesar), to Gentiles.

THE KINGDOM AND THE CHURCH

Clearly there is a connection between the kingdom and the church, but the two are not the same. The kingdom is not a way of looking at or describing the church.

The church is the assembly of all people who belong to Christ – those alive on earth and those already with him in heaven. The kingdom is the whole activity of God in Christ in the world.

Christ is central to both the kingdom and the church. However, 'the church' draws our attention to the results of his activity – to the bride, the body, and so on; whereas 'the kingdom' focuses us on him personally and his activity.

2 Peter 1:11 ☐

Revelation 1:9 ☐
11:15 ☐
12:10 ☐

Acts 1:3 ☐

Acts 17:7 ☐

The church is the assembly of those who have accepted the gospel of the kingdom, who participate in the salvation of the kingdom and look forward to the inheritance of the kingdom. But the church is not the kingdom.

However, Christian believers – who make up the church – are those in whom the kingdom takes its visible form. We are the light of the world, the salt of the earth, those who live by the king's rule and learn only from him. As such, the church is a tool of the kingdom: we carry out the kingdom's activities by living under the rule of God.

The church is called to preach the kingdom to the world and to pray for the kingdom to come in glory. The church should always be directed by the kingdom, yet it never becomes the kingdom.

If we put this another way, we can say that we are meant to be ruled by God, but we are not – and never can be – the rule of God. Many errors in church thinking and practice have arisen through confusing the church with the kingdom.

The kingdom has come. Christ is king. And he is as much a king where the church is weak and feeble as where it is strong and thriving. His kingship does not depend on the state of the church, for it is his by right. Instead, the church relies on the kingdom.

Every member of the church, every expression of the church, needs to be living in the kingdom – to be ruled only by God in Christ. The rest of this book is simply taken up with examining and applying what this means today.

PART TWO

the call of the kingdom

After John the Baptist had been put into prison, Jesus went into Galilee and began proclaiming the good news of God. According to Mark 1:14–15, this was the content of his good news, 'The time is fulfilled, and the kingdom of God is at hand. Repent and believe the gospel'.

Matthew 3:1 & 4:17 describe much the same message at the start of both John's and Jesus' ministry. This suggests that the coming of the kingdom was not an event which merely had to be announced, its coming was a challenge to which people had to respond.

For both John the Baptist and Jesus, the coming of the kingdom of God was such a significant event that people had to be called to change the way that they thought and the way they behaved. Jesus announced the kingdom's arrival in clear and simple language.

1. The time has come. The age of God's personal rule is beginning.

2. You are called to make a radical, personal response to the presence of God's personal rule.

3. God requires you to surrender totally to God's personal rule. This means that you must repent and believe.

Mark 1:14–15 ☐

Matthew 3:1 ☐
4:17 ☐

THE CALL TO REPENT

As John and Jesus make it plain that the primary call of the kingdom is 'repent', we must ensure that we know exactly what this word means.

Many believers associate 'repent' and 'repentance' with a change of behaviour. They think that it means stopping doing wrong deeds and being sorry for the wrong deeds. However, the New Testament uses Greek words which mean a change of mind, not a change of behaviour.

Metanoia

Metanoeo is the verb which means 'to repent' and *metanoia* is the noun for 'repentance'. Both words are made by combining *meta* – which means 'after' or 'change' – with *nous* – which means 'mind'.

It is vital we grasp what biblical repentance really means. It is a radical transformation of thought, attitude, outlook and direction. Repentance is mental revolution. It means changing our mind about God, changing our ideas about his nature and rule, changing the way we think about Jesus, sin, holiness and ourselves. Repentance simply means stopping thinking our way and starting to think like God.

We have seen that the Jews had many wrong ideas about the kingdom. We know that they had many false assumptions about the Messiah. The call for repentance in the context of the announcement of the kingdom's arrival was a call for a fundamental change of mind. For most people, nothing is harder.

Nacham

In the Old Testament, the Hebrew word *nacham* is usually translated as 'repent'. *Nacham* is hardly ever used to describe men and women 'repenting', instead it normally describes God repenting. We can see this in Genesis 6:6; Exodus 13:17; 32:14; Judges 21:6, 15; 1 Samuel 15:35; Job 42:6; Jeremiah 20:16; Amos 7:3, 6.

These passages are hard to understand if we think that repentance means 'stopping doing evil deeds'; they are easier when we realise that repentance means 'changing our mind' – which is what God did according to passages like Genesis 18:16–33 and Jonah 3:10.

Genesis 6:6 ☐

Exodus 13:17 ☐

32:14 ☐

Judges 21:6 ☐

21:15 ☐

1 Samuel 15:35 ☐

Job 42:6 ☐

Jeremiah 20:16 ☐

Amos 7:3–6 ☐

Genesis 18:16–33 ☐

Jonah 3:10 ☐

However, we must appreciate that whenever God does change his mind it is always consistent with his unchanging nature and purpose. For example, his 'repentance' in Jonah 3 reflects his eternal desire to bless those who turn to him.

Sub

In older translations, the Hebrew word *sub* is often translated as 'repentance' when men and women are the subject of the action. But *sub* literally means 'to turn' or 'to change direction' rather than 'to change the mind'. It is used in the Old Testament for turning to God.

The most common Old Testament way of expressing this is by turning to God 'with all the heart, soul and might'. We can see this in 2 Kings 17:13; 23:25; 2 Chronicles 6:26; 7:14; 15:4; 30:6; Nehemiah 1:9; Psalms 78:34; Isaiah 19:22; 55:7; Jeremiah 3:12, 14, 22; 18:8; Ezekiel 18:21; 33:11, 14; Daniel 9:13; Hosea 14:1,2; Joel 2:13; Jonah 3:10; Zechariah 1:3–4 & Malachi 3:7.

Sub describes a positive mental action. It does not primarily mean stopping doing something; rather it essentially means positively turning to God with every essence of our being. We know that turning to God involves turning from sinful thoughts, attitudes and actions – but these are the consequences of turning to God, not the cause.

Epistrepho

The Greek word *epistrepho* is the New Testament equivalent of *sub*. This word also means 'to turn' and is often translated as 'convert' in older versions of the Bible.

Acts 3:19 & 26:20 show that repentance and conversion – turning to God – are linked but different. Conversion is the whole process of turning to God; repentance is just one part of that process.

Conversion describes the act of turning to embrace God with every part of our being. Repentance describes a mental revolution, a fundamental change in our thinking, values and ideas.

Those who suggest that repentance primarily means 'stopping sinning' are not merely mistaken about the meaning of a Greek word, they are also implicitly suggesting that salvation is attained by human effort rather than received by God's grace through faith.

2 Kings 17:13 ☐
23:25 ☐

2 Chronicles 6:26 ☐
7:14 ☐
15:4 ☐
30:6 ☐

Nehemiah 1:9 ☐

Psalms 78:34 ☐

Isaiah 19:22 ☐
55:7 ☐

Jeremiah 3:12 ☐
3:14, 22 ☐
18:8 ☐

Ezekiel 18:21 ☐
33:11, 14 ☐

Daniel 9:13 ☐

Hosea 14:1,2 ☐

Joel 2:13 ☐

Jonah 3:10 ☐

Zechariah 1:3–4 ☐

Malachi 3:7 ☐

Acts 3:19 ☐
26:20 ☐

The teaching that repentance means stopping sinning and starting to behave differently leads both to legalism and disappointment. We have seen that the coming of God's kingdom – his personal rule – is meant to release us from all laws, so the kingdom call to repentance cannot mean something which contradicts the very essence of the kingdom.

Of course, Christian repentance should always bear fruit. Luke 3:8–14 makes this clear – and offers some challenging ideas about the fruit which is expected. But the three examples John describes are fruit which follow from repentance: they are not examples of repentance.

We can see this distinction in Romans 12:2. Instead of conforming to this world, we should be transformed by the renewing of our mind. Although Paul does not use the word 'repentance' here, he describes a mental revolution which is the key to knowing God's will, to being liberated from the world's way of thinking and behaving, and to bearing fruit in transformed living. It is this inner revolution in disciples' thinking, attitudes and direction that leads to the changed lives which bear fruit as they submit to God's personal rule.

Repentance in the New Testament

The wider New Testament use of *metanoia* helps us to understand repentance more fully.

- Jesus began his ministry with a call to repentance – Matthew 4:17.

- Jesus ended his ministry by urging that the call to repentance should be preached to all nations – Luke 24:47.

- Jesus taught that repentance was necessary for salvation – Luke 13:3–5.

- Jesus sent out the twelve to call for repentance – Mark 6:12.

- Jesus called sinners, not the righteous, to repent – Luke 5:32.

- There is joy in heaven when sinners repent – Luke 15:7, 70.

- Peter corrected his Pentecost listeners' wrong ideas about Jesus and called the enquirers to repentance – Acts 2:38.

- Paul challenged the Athenians' ideas about God and told them that the true God commands all people to repent – Acts 17:30.

- In his farewell message to the Ephesian leaders, Paul summed up his message as 'repentance towards God' – Acts 20:21.

- The revolution in thinking – repentance – is not self-effort. It is a gift from God – Acts 5:31; 11:18.

- Repentance is linked with the two gifts from God of forgiveness and of eternal life – Luke 24:47; Acts 2:38; 3:19; 5:31; 11:18.

Acts 20:21 ☐
Acts 5:31 ☐
11:18 ☐
Luke 24:47 ☐
Acts 2:38 ☐
3:19 ☐
5:31 ☐
11:18 ☐

We can see from these verses there is no doubt that repentance is an essential requirement for those people who are to become followers of Jesus – precisely because it is a duty for all people. Until people repent – until they change their mind (or have it changed by God) about themselves and God – they are not aware that they need to be saved.

What Jesus came to do in his life and death can only be applied by people who recognise both their own inability to save themselves and their need for a new relationship with God. This change of mind about our own condition and God's nature is not enough in itself, but it is an integral initial part of conversion.

THE CALL TO BELIEVE

When we grasp that the first kingdom call 'repent' means 'change your mind', it starts to become clear why 'believe' is the second call of the kingdom. Any change of mind must automatically involve starting to believe new things. If there is no new believing, there cannot have been any change of mind – any repentance.

For many people, 'believing' is an intellectual act. But 'belief' in the New Testament involves action; it is the application of repentance.

Faith and belief

The Greek word in the New Testament for 'to believe' is *pisteuo*, and this means 'to be persuaded of', 'to place confidence in', 'to trust'. *Pisteuo* means relying and depending as well as thinking. The Greek word *pistis* is normally translated as 'faith' – so we can quickly see that 'to believe' and 'to have faith' are just two different ways of expressing the same Greek idea. 'To believe' is simply the verbal form of the noun 'faith'.

Mark 1:15 ☐

According to Mark 1:15, Jesus' first words in ministry linked faith/belief and repentance. In view of the coming of the kingdom, he says that belief in the gospel must be added to repentance.

To believe in the gospel means to believe in Jesus himself. The people listening to Jesus were expected to commit themselves to all that Jesus stood for – for his whole mission. They were to believe in – to rely on – to depend on – to trust in – to have faith in – Jesus.

The gospels record a whole series of challenges to faith:

- Immediately after Mark 1:15, the first disciples are called to leave their fishing and follow Jesus.

Matthew 8:10, 13 ☐
9:22, 29 ☐
15:28 ☐

Mark 9:24 ☐
10:52 ☐

Luke 7:50 ☐
17:19 ☐

Matthew 8:26 ☐

Mark 4:40 ☐

Luke 8:25 ☐

Matthew 17:20 ☐
21:21–22 ☐

Luke 17:5 ☐

Mark 9:23 ☐

- Many of the healing miracles are the direct result of faith – Matthew 8:10, 13; 9:22, 29; 15:28; Mark 9:24; 10:52; Luke 7:50; 17:19.

- The disciples are rebuked for their lack of faith – Matthew 8:26; Mark 4:40; Luke 8:25.

- Jesus promises remarkable achievements to people of faith – Matthew 17:20; 21:21–22; Luke 17:5.

- Faith asserts possibilities in the face of impossibilities – Mark 9:23.

All these instances of faith are examples of the kingdom need to believe in – to depend on – the power of Jesus. His entire mission is based on the conviction that what God expects of people is impossible through human effort, but possible when faith links us to God's special way of doing things. This 'possibility' is understandable only when it centres on Jesus. It is in Christ that God does the impossible. It is through Christ that God rules in person.

Belief in John's Gospel

John 20:30–31 ☐

John 20:30–31 shows that the main purpose of John's gospel is that we might 'believe'. This gospel is packed with over one hundred statements about believing.

Interestingly, John always uses the verb *pisteuo* and never the noun *pistis*. Nobody really knows why John writes like this, but it is likely that it is his way of stressing the act of believing over the content of the belief. Throughout John's gospel, faith always involves a relationship – it is never just an intellectual assent to a creed.

In John's gospel, belief is occasionally seen in terms of accepting the message – believing that what Jesus said is true. However, belief is always directed at Jesus and usually involves trusting him personally – as in John 4:50; 8:30; 12:11; 14:1. Belief is sometimes prompted by the works Jesus did – for example, John 2:11 & 10:38. But Jesus usually requests belief in himself from his followers – as in 14:1 & 10.

John 1:12 makes it plain that salvation comes as a result of belief. Faith or belief is the means by which people are brought into the kingdom. This means that there is a clear distinction between believers and the world. In 3:16–17, faith secures eternal life and the lack of faith leads to condemnation.

We know that belief in Jesus begins in the radical transformation of mind called repentance. John does not mention 'repentance', but he vividly describes the change of mind needed for belief – although it does not inevitably lead to belief. The crowds at the feeding of the 5,000 in 6:22–59 saw nothing more than physical bread. But when – in 6:60–66 – they finally recognised that Jesus' view of life was different from their own, many of them rejected him.

Belief is essentially a human response to God's invitation. He presents his Son to us and we are bound to make some sort of decision about him. John's gospel uses different terms to express this response in 5:24; 6:40; 6:45; 8:43, 47; 12:45, 47; 14:7, 9; 17:23 & 18:37. If we receive Jesus, obey him, see him, know him, and so on, our response is positive. But if we do not respond in these ways, we do not believe – we do not have faith. We have rejected God's personal rule.

Belief in the early church

In Acts, belief is again shown as the natural development of repentance. In fact, in Acts 2:44; 4:4; 4:32; 9:42; 11:21; 14:23, the first Christian community was called 'those who believe'. As we should expect, the object of the people's faith is usually Jesus himself – as in Acts 11:17; 14:23; 16:31; 19:4; 20:21 & 24:24. Though sometimes they believe the word preached – as in 4:4 & 17:1–12.

Personal belief in Jesus was the distinguishing mark of Christians. They not only had to change their minds about him, they also had to

John 4:50 ☐
8:30 ☐
12:11 ☐
14:1 ☐
2:11 ☐
10:38 ☐
14:1 &10 ☐
1:12 ☐
3:16–17 ☐

John 6:22–66 ☐

John 5:24 ☐
6:40 ☐
6:45 ☐
8:43, 47 ☐
12:45, 47 ☐
14:7, 9 ☐
17:23 ☐
18:37 ☐

Acts 2:44 ☐
4:4 ☐
4:32 ☐
9:42 ☐
11:21 ☐
14:23 ☐
11:17 ☐
14:23 ☐
16:31 ☐
17:1–12 ☐
19:4 ☐
20:21 ☐
24:24 ☐

trust, believe, depend on Christ himself before they could appropriate what he had done for them through his death and resurrection. The whole process of conversion is dealt with much more fully in the *Sword of the Spirit* books about *Faith* and *Salvation*.

Romans 10:17 ☐

1 Corinthians
1:21 ☐

Ephesians 1:13 ☐

Romans 3:22–25 ☐

Romans 1:17 ☐

Galatians 2:20 ☐

In Romans 10:17; 1 Corinthians 1:21 & Ephesians 1:13, faith is the human response to the preaching of the gospel. But it is always faith in Christ, who has meaning only through faith.

Faith or belief is not just the initial act of accepting God's free gift of salvation – as in Romans 3:22–25 – it is also a continuous process. Just as we are called to go on repenting – to be characterised by the constant renewing of our minds – so too we are called to live by faith. Romans 1:17 & Galatians 2:20 express this progressive nature of faith.

When people are called to believe, they are not called simply to accept an act of Christ; they are also called to establish a new relationship with Christ which is characterised by belief – by relying, depending, trusting only in Christ. This naturally leads on to the third call of the kingdom.

THE CALL TO DISCIPLESHIP

Mark 1:15–20 ☐

Mark 1:15–20 shows how Jesus moved on from announcing the kingdom's arrival, through calling people to repent and believe in the gospel, to call specific people personally to follow him. Exactly the same progression is recorded in Matthew 4:17–22.

Matthew 4:17–22 ☐

When we start to believe in Jesus, we find that he calls us to demonstrate our belief by following him – by becoming a disciple.

The call is personal

The Greek word for disciple is *mathetes*, which literally means a 'learner'. *Mathetes* comes from *manthano* – 'to learn' – and shows that reflective thought should be followed by an attempt actually to do something. *Mathetes* reveals that real disciples are not people who obey unthinkingly or legalistically; rather, they listen to a teacher, think about what the teacher has said, and then try to put it into practice.

It should be clear how this concept of discipleship naturally follows on from a biblical understanding of repentance and belief. In Matthew 11:28–30, Jesus calls us to learn from him personally – this is true discipleship. Just as he does not call us to follow a set of ideas or rules but to follow him, so he does not call us to learn from the Law or a book but rather to learn from him himself.

Matthew 11:28–30 ☐

The call is urgent

The Gospels record many stories about people who were called to follow Jesus – to become disciples. In every one the call is most urgent. They had to respond when he asked them, even if that involved considerable disruption to them and the people around them. For example,

- Simon, Andrew, James and John – Matthew 4:18–22

  Matthew 4:18–22 ☐

- Matthew – Matthew 9:9

  Matthew 9:9 ☐

- the rich young man – Matthew 19:21

  Matthew 19:21 ☐

- an unnamed person – Luke 9:59

  Luke 9:59 ☐

- Philip – John 1:43

  John 1:43 ☐

We can see in these stories that some people immediately began following Jesus, but that others made excuses and did not. The calls of the kingdom may be compelling but they are not compulsory. God always wants us to respond in love. He does not make us if we will not follow him on his terms, at his time.

The call is conclusive

Not only was the call urgent, but it was conclusive. They were called permanently to forsake all and follow him.

- Luke 9:62 shows that there was to be no looking back.

  Luke 9:62 ☐

- Mark 10:33 states that Jesus must not be disowned before men.

  Mark 10:33 ☐

- John 8:31 makes it plain that disciples must hold to Jesus' teaching.

  John 8:31 ☐

Becoming a follower or disciple of Jesus is not merely an emotional response or mental assent to his teaching – it is a permanent decision to follow Jesus, to learn from him, to obey him, to keep close to him.

The call is costly

Mark 1:16–20 □

Luke 5:1–11 □

Luke 14:25–33 □

Matthew 6:33 □

Luke 12:31–34 □

Matthew
16:13–33 □

Mark 8:34 □

Luke 9:23 □

Mark 1:16–20 & Luke 5:1–11 tell the story of the calling to discipleship of the four fishermen, Simon, Andrew, James and John. By following Jesus' direction, they caught such a large number of fish that their nets were in danger of breaking and their boats of sinking.

Luke 5:11 reports that 'they forsook all and followed him'. The 'all' must have included the miraculous catch which they had just laboured to bring to shore. It must have been one of their most successful fishing trips ever, yet – as part of their response to Jesus – they left the catch on the beach for their friends and family.

Luke 14:25–33 describes how great multitudes went with Jesus. They were curious; they were interested – even fascinated; but they were not committed and they had not counted the cost.

In this passage, we can see that the essence of being a disciple was absent – they had not reflected and thought carefully about what was involved in following Jesus. Unless they would forsake everything they could not be Jesus' disciples.

Matthew 6:33 shows that we must put the kingdom of God first. Before everything else, we must seek God's rule and his right way of living. The parallel passage, in Luke 12:31–34, shows that this right living is characterised by selfless generosity.

When, in Matthew 16:13–33, the disciples realised who Jesus was, he explained to them that this meant suffering and death. This was anathema to the disciples, so Peter took Jesus aside and remonstrated with him. But Jesus rebuked them, said that their well-meaning protests were evil in origin, and told them that the divine demand for self-sacrifice applied to them as well as to him.

He said, in Matthew 16:24 and Mark 8:34, 'If anyone desires to come after me, let him deny himself, and take up his cross, and follow me'. Luke 9:23 adds that this must be done 'every day'.

These words were spoken to those who had already begun to follow Jesus, who had seen God work powerfully through them, who now grasped that Jesus was heading for rejection and sacrifice. Now that they knew the truth, Jesus set them free to choose between self and self-sacrifice.

To be a disciple is to say every day 'death to self'. This is not a set of ascetic exercises, instead it is being unaware of ourselves and aware only of Christ. It is putting Christ's will in place of 'self'. It is having our eyes so fixed on the one we are following that we are blind to the path which is too steep for us and deaf to the pain which pleads with us to stop. It means knowing that nothing in this life compares with the glory awaiting us – if we stick close to Jesus' bent and beaten back.

When we follow Christ, we must show that we mean death to self by taking up our God-offered cross. This is not an ailment or difficulty which is no different from those which are endured by all people. It will be some form of sacrifice, hardship or rejection 'for the sake of Christ' which is given to all those who follow him.

Each disciple who wants to follow in Christ's footsteps has his own personal cross awaiting collection. Each follower is meant to consider themselves to have the same short life-expectancy as the people who live on the different 'Death Rows' round the world.

This self-death is not a calamity, but the fruit of commitment. It is not the end of everything, rather it is the beginning of abundant life with Christ – as we begin to allow his will to control and rule us. The twelve heard these new requirements of discipleship, and not one of them walked away.

THE CALL TO BE CHRIST-LIKE

There is an obvious progression in the call of the kingdom. We are called to change the way that we think about God and Jesus and ourselves – to start thinking in God's way, to have his attitude and direction. Then we are called to believe in Jesus, to rely on him and trust him completely.

We show that we trust him by following him and becoming his disciples. We think about his words; we personally learn from him; and then we act on what he says.

But that is not the end. We are not merely called to follow him, we are also called – by following him – to become like him.

The Gospels record five key ways in which all disciples are called to be like Christ.

1.   Loving

In John 13:34, Jesus told the disciples that he had a new commandment for them. It was 'that you love one another as I have loved you.' The next verse shows that this love would prove to 'all' that they were Jesus' disciples.

John 13:34–35 ☐

This command was given just moments after Jesus had washed the disciples' feet, so the command to love one another in Jesus' way must be understood in terms of practical, menial service.

A little while later, in John 15:12, Jesus returns to the same theme. Once again he commands them to love each other as he loves them.

John 15:12 ☐

There are many believers who think that they are called to love Jesus – and they are; but loving like Jesus means loving *each other* in a thoroughly practical way. Verse 11 shows that this is the way to our joy being full.

2.   Giving

In John 15:13–14, Jesus explains exactly what he means by loving. It is sacrificial giving. It is laying down our lives for our friends.

John 15:13–14 ☐

Please note that, if we love each other as sacrificially as Jesus does, we are not merely called his disciples, we are now also identified as his 'friends'.

Verse 14 is very important. We are Jesus' friends when we do whatever he commands us. This is the personal rule of God in practice. This is kingdom living.

We have no idea what Jesus will command us – and we have even less idea what he will command others. It will be personal and unique to each person. However, we can expect that it will involve the loving, sacrificial giving which is the context of these words.

John 15:16 ☐

Verse 16 contains a wonderful promise. But we dare not divorce it from its surrounding verses. This promise is for the friends of Jesus who love and give in his way – for those followers who have become truly Christ-like.

3. Serving

Mark 10:45 is a key revelation about Jesus. Jesus had always claimed to be 'the Son of Man' – a name which carried powerful kingdom imagery for Jews.

Mark 10:45 ☐

This title comes from Daniel 7:13–14 where the Son of Man is given 'dominion and glory and a kingdom, that all peoples, nations and languages should serve him. His dominion is an everlasting dominion which shall not pass away, and his kingdom is the one which shall not be destroyed.'

Daniel 7:13–14 ☐

By claiming to be the Son of Man, Jesus was implicitly claiming to be the one whom Daniel was writing about. Yet, in Mark 10:45, Jesus turned the popular understanding of the Son of Man upside down.

Jesus said that, instead of being served by all people, 'The Son of Man did not come to be served, but to serve and to give his life a ransom for many.'

Jesus spoke these words to his disciples as the conclusion and explanation of his command in Mark 10:42–44 to serve in an entirely different way to the world. 'It shall not be so among you; but whoever desires to become great among you shall be your servant. And whoever of you desires to be first shall be the slave of all.'

Mark 10:42–44 ☐

We are to serve in exactly the same way as the Son of Man. As subjects of the king, we are called to serve Jesus – but this means serving others like Jesus, and serving them with Jesus.

Paul picks up this theme in Philippians 2:5–11. But we must make sure we note that Paul introduces this picture of Jesus the servant by urging us to 'let this mind be in you which was also in Christ Jesus'. Once again, we have to have God's attitudes – to think his way – before we can behave like him.

Philippians 2:5–11 ☐

4. Working

Jesus' words in John 14:12 are related to all this. 'He who believes in me, the works that I do he will do also; and greater works than these he will do, because I go to my Father'.

John 14:12 ☐

There are consequences to belief. If we think like Jesus; if we trust and rely on him; if we follow him, it is surely only to be expected that we will find ourselves doing the works that he does.

Many people's minds leap to miracles when they think about this verse and the works of Jesus. But this verse is set in the same foot-washing, laying down lives context as his commands to give and to love and to serve.

If we believe in Christ we can expect to behave like Christ. This will include mighty miracles, but it will be dominated by lowly service.

5.   Going

John 20:19–22 ☐

Jesus' first words to his disciples after his resurrection are recorded in John 20:19–22. Verse 21 contains his final call to be like him, 'As the Father has sent me, I also send you'.

John 5:19 ☐
     5:30 ☐
     6:38 ☐
     7:28–29 ☐
     8:26 ☐
     8:28–29 ☐
     10:18 ☐
     12:49–50 ☐

In John's Gospel, Christ constantly reveals himself as one who is sent, as one who is so under the personal rule of God that he says nothing of his own, does nothing of his own and goes nowhere on his own initiative. We can trace this through John 5:19, 30; 6:38; 7:28–29; 8:26, 28–29; 10:18 & 12:49–50. The Son speaks what the Father says. He does what the Father does. And he goes where the Father sends.

In exactly the same way, Jesus sends his disciples. They are to go as he has gone. This has two implications. Firstly, that disciples cannot stay where they are – there must be movement and action, there must be some 'going'. And secondly, that disciples 'go' under the personal rule of God. We should go only where he sends and when he sends – to say only what he says and do only what he does.

THE CALL TO INHERIT THE KINGDOM

Our Christ-like loving, giving, serving, working and going is not unrewarded. Jesus makes it plain that there is an ample inheritance and many rewards before us.

We have seen that there is a tension in the kingdom between now and not yet. All the kingdom calls we have examined have been part of the 'now' dimension of the kingdom. The call to repent and believe, to follow and become Christ-like is always for now – today, everyday. It is always a message for the present.

However, the last call of the kingdom looks forward to the day when the kingdom will finally be fully revealed and eternally established. The New Testament is packed with verses of kingdom promise. Some are conditional promises – rewards for particular godly behaviour. Others are unconditional – for all who believe. A few embrace the present, but they mostly look to the 'not yet' dimension of the kingdom.

- Matthew 5:5 – the earth

- Matthew 5:10 – the kingdom of heaven

- Matthew 6:19–21 – treasure in heaven

- Matthew 10:40–42 – a righteous man's reward

- Matthew 19:27–30 – a hundredfold

- Matthew 25:31–40 – the prepared kingdom

- Luke 6:30–38 – a great reward

- Luke 12:32 – the kingdom, heavenly treasure

- Luke 14:12–14 – repaid with blessing

- Luke 16:9 – everlasting habitations

- Acts 20:32; 26:18 – an inheritance

- Romans 2:6–10 – glory, honour and peace

- Romans 8:10 – a share of Christ's glory

- 2 Corinthians 9:6–14 – a bountiful harvest

- Ephesians 1:17–19 – the riches of the glory of his inheritance

- Ephesians 2:4–8 – the exceeding riches of his grace

- Colossians 3:23 – the reward of the inheritance

- 2 Timothy 2:12 – reign with Christ

- Hebrews 6:12 – the promises

- Revelation 3:21 – to sit with Christ on his throne

- Revelation 21:7 – all things

Matthew 5:5 ☐
5:10 ☐
6:19–21 ☐
10:40–42 ☐
19:27–30 ☐
25:31–40 ☐

Luke 6:30–38 ☐
12:32 ☐
14:12–14 ☐
16:9 ☐

Acts 20:32 ☐
26:18 ☐

Romans 2:6–10 ☐
8:10 ☐

2 Corinthians
9:6–14 ☐

Ephesians
1:17–19 ☐
2:4–8 ☐

Colossians 3:23 ☐

2 Timothy 2:12 ☐

Hebrews 6:12 ☐

Revelation 3:21 ☐
21:7 ☐

Some people mistakenly think that all the Bible teaching about inheritance automatically follows on from our salvation. But a careful reading of these verses shows that the inheritance is not received simply by believing – it is the reward for living under God's rule.

Matthew 19:23–
20:16 ☐

A passage like Matthew 19:23–20:16 proves that inheritance is reward. In answer to Peter's 'What shall we have?' in verse 27, Jesus speaks about inheritance. Verse 30 shows that there will be many surprises, and the following parable again teaches about surprising and controversial rewards.

One call of the kingdom may be 'forsake all and follow Christ', but an echo soon returns promising wonderful heavenly rewards for those disciples who do forsake all. We may not experience many of these rewards in this life, but they are all guaranteed by the very name of God at the last day.

PART THREE

the attitudes of the kingdom

Matthew
5:1–7:29 ☐

The Sermon on the Mount, in Matthew 5:1–7:29, is probably the best known part of Jesus' teaching. Yet it is also, perhaps, the least understood section.

This sermon is the first of Matthew's five blocks of teaching – the others are 10; 13; 18 & 24–25. We have seen that Matthew writes particularly for Jews: this use of five blocks of teaching parallels the five books of the Pentateuch (Genesis to Deuteronomy) and suggests that Jesus is a second Moses.

Moses brought God's rules to the people of Israel, but Matthew shows that Jesus has fulfilled the Law and is now bringing a new and better way of regulating living for God's people – the kingdom of heaven or God's personal rule.

Throughout the sermon, Jesus authoritatively unfolds the key principles of his kingdom and sets out the standards he expects from his subjects. To underline their authority, some of his sayings are introduced with the solemn Hebrew word *Amen*, which means 'verily' or 'in truth'. This note of personal authority is enhanced by Jesus' repeated use of 'I tell you' or 'I say to you'.

It is vital we grasp that the Sermon is not:

- rules for non-Christian society

- the means of entering the kingdom

- a new Christian law

Matthew 5:1–2 ☐

Instead, 5:1–2 shows that it is Jesus' teaching for those who are already his disciples, for those who have already heard the call of the kingdom and forsaken all to follow him. The sermon is a description of God's radical alternative life-style for those disciples who have obeyed his 'follow me' and have begun to live under God's personal rule. Throughout this book, we will see that this life-style:

- glorifies God

- challenges the world

- brings rewards

Matthew 6:9–13 ☐

God's personal rule is central throughout. For example, the sermon includes the Lord's Prayer, 6:9–13, with its distinctive phrase, 'Your kingdom come' and the immediate explanation, 'Your will be done on earth'. And it ends with Jesus' explanation that only those disciples who do the will of the Father will enter the kingdom of heaven, 7:21.

Matthew 5:3–12 ☐

The Sermon on the Mount sets out the attitudes – not the actions – which characterise true disciples. The introduction to the sermon, 5:3–12, is usually called 'the beatitudes', and this is a list of eight basic attitudes which Jesus develops, illustrates and explains throughout the rest of his sermon.

Each 'beatitude' begins with the Greek word *makarios* – which is usually translated as either 'blessed' or 'happy'. *Makarios* is nothing to do with 'blessings'. Instead, it comes from the Greek word *mak* which means 'large' or 'lengthy' and carries the idea of someone with a big

Luke 1:48 ☐

smile on their face. It is the word used by Mary in Luke 1:48 and is best understood by 'very fortunate' or even 'to be congratulated'.

The beatitudes or 'beautiful attitudes' give a general character description of those disciples who are living 'in the kingdom'. As we read them, we see what we are meant to look like as a result of God's personal rule in our life. If we live fully under the personal rule of God, we can expect to be characterised by these attitudes.

1. POOR IN SPIRIT

There is a strict and important order to the attitudes. 'How fortunate are the poor in spirit, for the kingdom of heaven is theirs' comes first. The other seven attitudes, and the rest of the Sermon on the Mount, all follow on from this first and fundamental attitude.

Matthew 5:3 ☐

Nobody can be part of God's kingdom unless they are poor in spirit, for this is the basic characteristic of every true Christian. All the other characteristics are, in a sense, only a result of being poor in spirit.

When Jesus was a baby, Simeon told Mary and Joseph, in Luke 2:34, that the child would bring about 'the fall and rising of many'. Since then, it has been an important Christian principle that crucifixion comes before resurrection, that falling comes before rising; that the best is always still to come for those who are with Christ.

Luke 2:34 ☐

Poverty of spirit is the entry-point to God's kingdom, but just as the rise follows the fall, so the delights of the kingdom – the joy, fruit, inheritance and rewards – come to those, and only those, who are genuinely poor in spirit.

What is poverty of spirit?

When we read the Sermon on the Mount, we see famous phrases like:

- 'turn the other cheek' – 5:39

- 'don't worry about tomorrow' – 6:34

- 'love your enemies' – 5:44

- 'give to everyone who asks' – 5:42

Matthew 5:39 ☐
6:34 ☐
5:44 ☐
5:42 ☐

These are not new rules which mean expulsion from the kingdom if broken. They are not a code of law which results in fines or punishment when breached. Instead they are like a dazzlingly beautiful mountain which we long to climb, have been told we must climb, but which we know is utterly beyond us.

The sermon is something which is inescapably impossible to keep. Anyone who reads it and then tries to live it in their own strength shows that they have misunderstood it.

As with an incredibly high mountain, there is only one sensible reaction to the sermon – a longing look and a painful cry, 'I really want to do it, but I know that I can't! Will someone who can please help me?'

Whoever cries those words – or words like them – with deep sincerity shows that they are poor in spirit – and the kingdom of heaven is theirs.

Being poor in spirit means recognising that – as far as our relationship with God is concerned – we are utterly poverty stricken and bankrupt.

These passages help us to understand poverty of spirit more fully:

- Ephesians 2:1–10 – we know that we are dead in trespasses and sin
- Matthew 23:25–28 – we know that we are self-indulgent and hypocritical
- Isaiah 6:5 – we know that we have 'unclean lips'
- Luke 5:8 – we know that we are intrinsically sinful

It is not material poverty

Poverty of spirit is hard to describe, but obvious when seen. It is important we understand that it is not the same as being poor. Jesus does not say that the poor in material things are fortunate.

However, the poor may be more likely to be poor in spirit than the rich – which, perhaps, is one reason why the church is growing faster in poorer nations than in affluent ones.

We have seen that Jesus asks his followers to give up everything to follow him, and the poor have less to give up than the rich. Perhaps this explains Jesus' principle in Luke 18:25.

It is not popular

Poverty of spirit is not a popular idea in the world. Magazines and TV programmes do not offer advice on how to become poor in spirit today. Instead, the world advocates self-reliance, self-fulfilment and self-expression. The world's version of this beatitude could be 'How fortunate are the self-confident, for prosperity and popularity will be theirs'.

Ephesians 2:1–10 ☐

Matthew
            23:25–28 ☐

Isaiah 6:5 ☐

Luke 5:8 ☐

Luke 18:25 ☐

The world encourages people to 'believe in yourself'. Poverty of the spirit is the exact opposite. It is:

- the complete absence of pride
- to have no selfish ambition
- to possess no hint of self-assurance
- to be without any self-confidence

A man or woman is only poor in spirit when they carry with themselves at all times a total awareness of their utter nothingness when faced with the ultimate reality of God.

Jesus was poor in spirit

We know that Jesus fed thousands, stilled storms, healed the sick, raised the dead, cast out demons and taught with great authority. Yet we have also seen that he said he could do nothing by himself. This must be either a lie or the most revolutionary truth in the universe.

Jesus appeared to be able to do *anything*. But he knew the eternal and absolute truth that, by himself, he could do *nothing*. He knew that to go anywhere, to do anything, to help anyone, to achieve anything, he needed to rely on the all-powerful, all-loving God.

The apostles were poor in spirit

It was the same for the early church leaders. They were not weak people who were naturally retiring or lacking in courage. They did not try to create poverty of spirit by pretending to be humble or by boasting about their inadequacies.

Instead, they were so close to God they recognised that their natural abilities, formal qualifications, worldly status or good behaviour were to be regarded as a pile of dung and a hindrance to the better way of relying on God's personal rule.

We must be poor in spirit

It should be the same today. The poor in spirit are disciples who do not rely on their backgrounds, do not trust in their education, do not depend on their wealth or status. They know that, in comparison with God, these are as useful as a concrete parachute.

Disciples are not poor in spirit because they are inadequate or repressed. Instead, we become poor in spirit by spending time gazing at God and following Jesus – in this way we come to know what we are compared to them.

Through this basic characteristic, the poor in spirit become those who are considered fortunate – because theirs is the kingdom of heaven. 2 Corinthians 6:10 & 8:9 illustrate how all the blessings of the kingdom come to those with this foundation attitude.

2 Corinthians
   6:10 ☐
   8:9 ☐

2.   MOURNING

Matthew 5:4 ☐

Like the first attitude, the second one clearly shows that the central character of the kingdom is strikingly different from the normal attitude of the world today. It is totally absurd by human reasoning.

Society shuns mourning. The world organises lives to avoid mourning. People encourage each other to forget their troubles and put them behind them. Leisure centres, home entertainment and canned laughter are the fashion. Yet Jesus contradicts all this: 'How fortunate are those who mourn, for they will be comforted'.

Even churches have been affected by society's attitude. If Jesus visited some congregations today and urged them to mourn, the leaders would probably correct him and tell him to rejoice and be glad, to smile and be happy, to be joyful and praise God. However, Jesus said that those disciples who live under his rule would be characterised by an attitude which values mourning.

What is mourning?

Just as the first attitude was not about something financial but something essentially spiritual, so too this second attitude is more about spiritual mourning than natural mourning.

All eight attitudes refer to a spiritual condition and a spiritual attitude. This means that the people who are highly commended are those who mourn in spirit – they are the fortunate disciples who will be rewarded with the personal comfort of God.

Everybody mourns naturally at the sad moments of life, but few people mourn in spirit. And even fewer disciples of Jesus are characterised by a depth of mourning which reflects the way he mourned for Jerusalem, for the religious leaders of his day, and for his closest friends when they argued among themselves.

Those who mourn in spirit are those who weep with God about the things which make him cry. Paul calls this 'godly sorrow' in 2 Corinthians 7:10. They mourn for themselves, for their flawed humanity, for the good they want to do but do not do, and for the bad they do that they do not want to do. They recognise that they are like a cracked egg or a pizza which is just past its sell-by-date – still useful, but not as good as they should be. James 4:7–10 & Isaiah 6:5 set this in context.

2 Corinthians 7:10 ☐

James 4:7–10 ☐

Isaiah 6:5 ☐

What do we mourn about?

- We should mourn for our unwillingness to love our enemies, to give to everyone who asks, to turn the other cheek, and so on. We should mourn for our lack of embarrassment at collecting clothes, cars and electronic gadgets when we follow the one who told us to sell our possessions and give to poor. We should mourn because we recognise that we are like an imitation Rolex or a pair of Taiwanese trainers – useful, but not as good as the item we are modelled upon.

- We should mourn for God's polluted planet, for the human greed which destroys forests, poisons the atmosphere, sells weapons, fills rivers with pesticides and chokes people with exhaust fumes.

- We should mourn for human injustice: for debt and unfair trade practices, for homelessness and refugees, for the way that we treat the unborn, prisoners, the mentally ill and the elderly.

- We should mourn about social unrest, social fragmentation and the love of materialism which is the root of all evil; for our neighbour's apathy towards God and our apathy towards our neighbour's eternal destiny.

Psalm 119:136 ☐

This sort of mourning, which we see in Psalm 119:136, is not morbid or false or hypocritical. It is liberating, envisioning and a spur to Spirit-filled, God-directed social action. It is the most honest and accurate assessment of the people we are and the world that we live in – it is truly Christian thinking – it is genuine *metanoia*.

God's reward to mourners

Jesus promises that those disciples who mourn *now* will *one day* be comforted – that is why they are fortunate. If we mourn with God today, we will be comforted by the Comforter tomorrow.

Many disciples in heaven will not be comforted by God. Some create their own comfort on earth with artificial 'joy' and 'happy clappy' triumphalism. Others comfort themselves or choose the comfort of adulation or escapism. A few will not be comforted because they are too pre-occupied to mourn or have been taught not to mourn.

Isaiah 12:1–6 ☐

Psalm 30:5 ☐

32:1–2 ☐

Romans 4:7–8 ☐

But how fortunate are those who mourn spiritually because they will be comforted by God himself. As in Isaiah 12:1–6; Psalm 30:5; 32:1–2 & Romans 4:7–8, our godly sorrow will end in godly joy and rejoicing.

3. MEEKNESS

Matthew 5:5 ☐

Every day, battles rage as nations or people groups try to establish supremacy over part of the earth. Most people believe that 'might' will triumph over 'right' in the end, but Jesus suggests something different.

The third kingdom attitude states: 'How fortunate are the meek, for they shall inherit the earth'. World control, universal authority, possession of this planet – all of these will be given not to the strong or the powerful, nor to the wealthy or well-organised, but to the meek.

It seems absurd. It is the reverse of human experience and opposed to worldly thinking. Once again, Jesus shows how much we need a mental revolution to live in the kingdom. His way of thinking is fundamentally opposed to modern society.

Many churches agree with the world. They would like to be large and powerful so that they can dominate their part of the earth. They long to be heard on the media. They become assertive and pray for more power. And the one they pray to replies, 'How fortunate are the meek, for they – and only they – shall inherit the earth'.

The order of the attitudes

Jesus' eight attitudes follow a logical order. The poor in spirit begin to mourn when they become aware of the extent of their failings – and this awareness leads naturally on to meekness.

The first attitude asks us to admit our weakness and lack of ability. The second asks us not only to recognise our poverty of spirit but also to mourn for it. The third attitude – meekness – takes us further into God, towards the point where we stop being concerned about ourselves and start being concerned for others.

Many of us are happy to condemn ourselves but we do not like it when others point out our failings. The first two attitudes help Jesus' disciples to examine themselves honestly. Meek disciples go one step further and allow others to examine them as well.

What is meekness?

Philippians 2:5–11 shows that Jesus had the right to equality with God, but chose not to assert it and to follow the way of a slave instead. That is the attitude of meekness which his disciples are meant to possess – both before God and before each other.

- Meekness before God involves being grateful, devoted, contented and submitted to him.

- Meekness before humans involves being gentle, teachable and forgiving. We can see this in Philippians 4:5; Galatians 6:1; Matthew 11:28–30; Isaiah 50:4–5; 1 Corinthians 13:5; Romans 12:17–21 & 1 Peter 2:23.

Meek people are patient; they do not mind being overlooked or criticised; they allow others to take priority. They give in to others, never make demands and let others assert themselves.

Meek people are not weak people: they are strong people who live gently. They are not fools who are easily duped: they are wise people

Philippians
2:5–11 ☐

Philippians 4:5 ☐

Galatians 6:1 ☐

Matthew
11:28–30 ☐

Isaiah 50:4–5 ☐

1 Corinthians
13:5 ☐

Romans
12:17–21 ☐

1 Peter 2:23 ☐

Acts 8:32 ☐

John 13:5 ☐

Luke 10:3 ☐

Matthew 16:24 ☐

who respond humbly. They are not timid people who are afraid to speak up: they are articulate people who speak discreetly. They are not normal people who demand their own way: they are Jesus' people who always go God's way – his Acts 8:32; John 13:5; Luke 10:3 & Matthew 16:24 way.

Meek people do not worry about themselves or what people say about them – for they know that there is nothing worth defending. They do not waste time in self pity, because they have finished with themselves and know that they have no rights at all. Being poor in spirit, they know that nobody can say or do anything to them which is too bad – they know they deserve it and more.

The truly meek disciple is always amazed that God and other people can think of them as well as they do. And it is this essential meekness which enables us to see and to accept who we are in Christ.

Meekness' reward

Jesus promises that the meek will inherit the earth. In the 'now' dimension of the kingdom, this is already partly true. Meek people are satisfied and contented. They can enjoy things without wanting to own them. In one sense, they have already inherited the earth, for they alone are free to enjoy it without wanting to possess or control it.

Luke 14:11 ☐

Romans 8:17 ☐

1 Corinthians 2:9 ☐

2 Corinthians
        6:10 ☐

Revelation 21:7 ☐

However, this is another obvious 'not yet' kingdom promise – along the same lines as Luke 14:11; Romans 8:17; 1 Corinthians 2:9; 2 Corinthians 6:10 & Revelation 21:7. The fallen will rise. The last will be first. The crucified will be resurrected. The meek will inherit the earth. This is either a terrible deception or an amazing truth.

4.   HUNGRY FOR RIGHTEOUSNESS

Matthew 5:6 ☐

The first four attitudes underline the spiritual bankruptcy and over-whelming inadequacy felt by authentic disciples. Those who live under the rule of God are poor in spirit, they mourn, they are meek before God and other people, and now the fourth attitude shows us that they are empty and want to be filled. 'How fortunate are those who hunger and thirst for righteousness, for they shall be filled.'

Seeking happiness

The world is looking for *makarios*. It wants big smiles and good fortune. It is full of people who are seeking for happiness. But they are looking both in the wrong place and in the wrong way.

Jeremiah 2:13 shows that people have committed two acts of evil. Not only have they forsaken God – the source of living, continuous, flowing waters, they have also made for themselves tanks to contain and regulate water. But the tanks are broken, they do not work.

Jeremiah 2:13 ☐

God is the source of life, love, joy, satisfaction and contentment. We are made by him for him. We can only know true happiness in and through him – by depending on his supply of living water. Yet we have rejected him and tried to create alternative reservoirs of happiness. The world thinks it will find happiness by making it its priority. Jesus says that happiness is a by-product of seeking God's righteousness.

Hungry and thirsty

The fourth beatitude speaks of disciples being hungry and thirsty. Few Western Christians have ever known real natural hunger and thirst. We might miss a meal and feel a bit peckish. We might need a drink on a hot day and have to walk an extra mile to a stream or cafe. Our lives of comfort have devalued the words 'hunger' and 'thirst'.

Jesus is using words which describe complete desperation. His disciples should be marked by this sort of total pre-occupation. Only one thing matters. Everything else is secondary. They know that they are empty and are desperate to be filled. To be genuinely hungry and thirsty for something is to make that thing the highest priority and purpose in life, and to persist until it is attained.

What is righteousness?

True disciples who share Jesus' attitudes are hungry for righteousness – in the way that Psalm 27:4 describes. The Greek word used here is

Psalm 27:4 ☐

dikaiosune and this describes the character of 'being right with God'. It is a word which appears frequently in Matthew – 6.33 shows that it is a central characteristic of the kingdom.

Being righteous simply means 'conforming to God's rule or revealed will' – we can see this in Matthew 3:15; 5:6, 10, 20; 21:32: John 16:8, 10; Romans 6:12–23; Ephesians 6:14; James 1:20 & 3:18.

To be hungry for righteousness is to be hungry for God and thirsty to conform to God's will – to want to please God by living under his rule.

When are we filled?

Jesus' promise is that those who are hungry and thirsty for righteousness will be filled. He does not specify *what* they will be filled with, but it has to be the righteousness of God. The next four attitudes describe what this means in detail.

He also does not say *when* they will be filled – except that it has to be after they have begun to hunger and thirst. However, the New Testament shows that the 'now' and 'not yet' kingdom tension is again repeated.

- Romans 5:1 speaks about the gift of righteousness by which we are made right with God, and which every disciple has received.

- 2 Corinthians 3:9–18 describes a progressive increase in righteousness.

- 2 Peter 3:13 looks forward to the new heaven and new earth in which only righteousness exists.

5. MERCIFUL

The fifth attitude is another stage in the development of a truly Christ-like character. The first four underline our serious needs; now, with the fifth, the positive side of the character begins to emerge. 'How fortunate are the merciful, for they shall receive mercy.' Disciples who live under God's personal rule will be essentially merciful.

The final four attitudes are all based on the first four. In fact they are their direct consequence, for they are the character which develops in those disciples who see themselves honestly and know the basis of their relationship with God.

Jesus is always more concerned with his followers' attitudes than their actions, with their thoughts than their behaviour. So here, instead of commending those who do acts of mercy, he congratulates those who are full of mercy. They were filled at the end of the last attitude, now he reveals what they have been filled with.

Our actions express what we are – they demonstrate our inner attitudes; and disciples' lives are supposed to show mercy because nobody can be a disciple without having experienced God's mercy.

What is mercy?

Mercy is not an easy-going attitude which says that nothing matters, that laws are not important and people can do as they like. The mercy Jesus describes must be the opposite of this, as it is found in the people who have been filled with God's way of right being. Mercy is only authentic when it is set in the context of hungering for God's high standards and Jesus' perfect life.

A few believers seem to stop at the fourth attitude. They know God is just and holy. They know his standards and are hungry for them. But they become judgmental, not merciful. They may show God's righteousness, but they do not show his mercy – and so give a false picture of God to the world. Ephesians 2:4 shows how rich God is in mercy, and we should reflect this in our attitudes and actions.

Ephesians 2:4 ☐

Mercy is rather like grace. It describes the way God freely gives everything to undeserving people without any terms and conditions. Grace is linked to people in their sin, whereas mercy is associated with them in their suffering. Grace is the word for God's response to human sin as a whole; mercy is the word for the way he deals with the suffering which stems from sin.

Mercy is practical pity for the suffering of a particular person – *plus* a desire, an intention *and* an action to relieve that suffering. It is empathy mixed with action. It is what we read about in Luke 10:25–37 & Mark 1:40.

Luke 10:25–37 ☐

Mark 1:40 ☐

Of course, many ordinary people have this sort of feeling for those who are obviously needy. Jesus' mercy goes much further, for the suffering he pities and tries to relieve includes things which ordinary people long for – the miseries of materialism, affluence, power, greed and the other consequences of selfishness and sin.

They will be shown mercy

God is the only acceptable example. He gave humanity this planet. We ruined it. He gave us the freedom to love him. We rejected him. He sent his Son to show us his love. We crucified him. He sees our suffering, our misery, our ambition and our love of possessions. He hears our lies, our arrogance, our posturing and our trust in false wisdom. And he responds to all this with evermore grace and mercy.

The fortunate ones whom Jesus commends are those who have recognised exactly what they are like. They are poor in spirit – and he gives them his kingdom. They mourn – and he comforts them. They are meek – and he promises them the earth. They are hungry for his right being and doing – and he fills them to the top.

Surely our past and present experience of God's mercy will affect our attitude to others. Surely our awareness of our faults and failings will prompt us to react with mercy towards others who suffer because of similar human shortcomings.

We will begin to be filled with the attitude of mercy when we know how far we are eternally indebted to God's mercy – when we become deeply conscious of the fact that we are only what we are because of God's infinite grace.

A future experience

Although we all have experienced God's mercy, Jesus' promise of mercy here is set in the future. This shows that an attitude of mercifulness is not a condition of salvation – rather it is an evidence of discipleship.

This Christ-like quality – like so many others – attracts the blessing of God. It will be rewarded at the last day. If we refuse to show mercy – or any of the other kingdom attitudes – we will not lose our salvation, but we will invite our heavenly Father's displeasure.

6. PURE IN HEART

At first sight, the sixth attitude seems to be in the wrong place. 'How fortunate are the pure in heart, for they shall see God' is such a magnificent promise that it looks as though it should the first or the last on the list. But the attitudes are in a logical order. Each one follows on from the one before, each is harder than the one before – and we are called to press on through them all, right to the heart of God.

Matthew 5:8 ☐

Many disciples who are poor in spirit, who know that they are nothing compared to Jesus, go on to mourn for their failings. Some of those who mourn for the worst in themselves become meek before others and allow them to examine them too. Some of the meek are not content with their failings and go on to hunger and thirst for righteousness. Some disciples who taste God's grace and mercy become merciful to others. And some of those who are full of his mercy go on in the rule of God to become pure in heart.

Like the others, this attitude shows that Jesus is more concerned with internal than external matters. Jesus does not commend the pure in behaviour, because he is more concerned with character than conduct.

Neither does he commend purity of doctrine. The call of the kingdom and the first five attitudes might have led us to expect Jesus to commend 'the pure in intellect'. But Jesus says that the pure in heart are fortunate because they – and only they – will see God.

What is purity of heart?

In Jesus' day, the heart was a picture for the seat of human personality, the centre of a person's being, the inner, invisible 'me' mentioned in 1 Samuel 16:1 & 1 Peter 3:4. Jesus is referring to disciples who are pure in their thinking, emotions and wills – to those who are pure in the centre of their being, right at the source of their attitudes and emotions.

1 Samuel 16:1 ☐

1 Peter 3:4 ☐

One of scripture's central messages is 'get your heart right'. We see this in Proverbs 4:23 & Matthew 15:8. This means two things:

Proverbs 4:23 ☐

Matthew 15:8 ☐

- to be washed, scrubbed and made completely clean and undefiled

- to be without anything hidden, to be straightened out – honest, straightforward and single-minded

A vision of God

As with the other promises, this is slightly ambiguous. Jesus does not make it clear how, where or when the pure in heart will see God. He simply makes it clear that they will see him! We see this in 1 Timothy 1:17; 2 Timothy 6:16; 1 Corinthians 13:12 & 1 John 3:2.

Again, this is fulfilled partly 'now' and more fully 'then'. In one sense disciples already see God in a way that nobody else does – in creation, other people, events, believers, worship, the Scriptures and their everyday experience. All this is part of seeing God – but it is as nothing compared to the way the pure will see him in the future.

When we have an appointment to meet an important person, we take care to wash carefully, dress thoughtfully and prepare our words. When we grasp that we have the chance of seeing God, everything else will fade into insignificance. When we realise that we have the chance of seeing the King of kings, we will do our utmost to grasp it.

Only the pure in heart will see him, and no-one can make their heart pure. We can prevent it from being purified; we can hinder the process; but we cannot purify ourselves. That is God's work.

- He demands absolute purity – Psalm 24:4; Hebrews 12:14; Revelation 21:27.

- He provides inner purity – 1 John 1:7; Ezekiel 36:25–27; Hebrews 10:22; 1 Corinthians 6:11.

But Romans 8:5; Psalm 86:11; 2 Corinthians 6:17–7:1 & Ephesians 5:3–10 show that we must have a genuine 'heart-desire' for God. We must want to be ruled by God, to have his attitudes, to be like Jesus.

7. PEACEMAKERS

It is a basic feature of flawed humanity to want to control, to dominate, to be powerful. But this is not Jesus' way. He did not commend the warriors or the rulers, the powerful or the leaders, instead he said: 'How fortunate are the peacemakers, for they shall be called children of God'.

Only disciples who are poor in spirit enter fully into God's kingdom. A few are then paralysed by their awareness of their poverty, while the rest make spiritual progress and mourn for their failings. Some who begin in mourning end in moaning, the others become meek. One or two of the meek become passive and weak, but most go on to hunger for being right before God.

Sadly, a few of those who taste God's righteousness do become harsh; but the others are filled with mercy. Some merciful disciples settle for second best, but we are all called to progress to purity of heart. A few of the pure opt out of the world, but God wants us all to press on to reach the point where our attitudes become our actions, where our character shows itself in conduct, where our filling with and by God has a deeply practical Christ-like result.

It is important we understand that we can all progress through all the attitudes. The fact that a few believers do sometimes backslide does not mean that we are all bound to stagnate in our spiritual life. Jesus calls us to follow him, and he provides us with everything we need to follow him deeply into his wonderful kingdom. We can all reach the point where we are filled with his attitudes, so we must keep going along God's way – even when it is narrow and difficult.

These beautiful attitudes show that people who are filled with God have three positive characteristics – mercy, purity and peace-making. These are the key ingredients in disciples who are ruled by God.

Just as each attitude becomes harder, so each promise gets better. Those disciples who are peacemakers will be called 'children of God'. They will not just be clients, spectators, members, citizens, servants, partners or disciples – they will also be children. They will have a new identity to go with their new nature, and a new relationship which matches their attitudes.

What is peacemaking?

Peacemakers are not quarrelsome or argumentative. They do not go out of their way to make trouble. They are not concerned with themselves. Instead they go out of their way, at great personal cost, to bring people together in a peace-filled relationship which is based on God's justice.

Peacemakers are not over-sensitive or defensive. They do not look at situations and ask how they will affect them or their group. Instead they are pure, meek, humble. They are dead to self and self-interest – when they look at a situation they ask only how it will affect others.

Peacemakers must first mourn and be merciful. They look at people lost in their anger and bitterness and realise that they are the victims of selfishness and sin. They know that these people are heading for hell – and this increases their mourning and mercy. Then they do something.

Peacemakers are deeply practical people. They do all the things that the rest of the Sermon on the Mount describes:

- they make reconciliation a priority
- they go the extra mile
- they turn the other cheek
- they love their enemies
- they give to everyone who asks
- they keep their generosity and righteousness to themselves
- they serve God not money
- they set their hearts on God's kingdom
- they do not judge others
- they do not worry

In one sense, the rest of the Sermon on the Mount is only a lengthy description of practical peacemaking. It follows on from the beautiful attitudes and illustrates the consequences of being ruled by God – of living in his kingdom.

Right at the start, we saw that these hard sayings of Jesus are impossible to keep by self-effort, now we can see that they are the natural result of following Christ and progressing from poverty of spirit right through to his holy peace-making.

Children of God

Those disciples who make eternal and earthly peace their priority will be claimed by God as their children. This is why so many of the

Isaiah 52:7 ☐

Ephesians 6:15 ☐

Matthew 5:23–24 ☐
18:15–20 ☐

Ephesians 4:26 ☐

Bible's promises of heavenly rewards and inheritance are not for doctrine and dealing with demons, but for welcoming strangers, feeding the hungry and housing the homeless.

To be a child of God is to be a brother or sister of Jesus. He showed all the eight attitudes all of the time, but his highest priority was to make peace – peace between God and ourselves, and peace between people. He is 'the Prince of Peace' – the supreme peacemaker – and all those who follow him are meant to be like him.

8. PERSECUTED

The first seven attitudes have all underlined the fact that the kingdom is very different from the common sense of modern society. The eighth is an even bigger surprise: 'How fortunate are those who are persecuted in the cause of righteousness, for theirs is the kingdom of heaven'.

Matthew 5:10–12 ☐

Today, we feel sorry for those who are persecuted. We try to support them. We campaign for them. We sometimes admire them; but we do not envy them or think that they are fortunate. Jesus does – if they are persecuted for righteousness' sake.

The first seven attitudes describe disciples who are ruled by God. The final one is more the inevitable result of the seven than a separate attitude. However, it is an account of a genuine follower of Jesus.

The world will not come to Christianity on the basis of the attitudes. Mourning, meekness, mercy and purity are not attractive ideas to contemporary minds. Persecution is even less so. Jesus' suggestion that being filled with his attitudes is bound to lead to persecution seems destined to put most people off becoming a disciple for life. But Jesus always tells the full truth, and then leaves us to choose whether or not to follow him along his narrow way.

The reward

His promise to the persecuted is the same as his promise to the poor in spirit: the kingdom of heaven. By starting and finishing with the

Luke 10:17–20 ☐

same reward, he shows that deep involvement with his heavenly kingdom is his most important gift of all.

Jesus' disciples were often excited by the crowds' adulation. However, Jesus told them, in Luke 10:17–20, not to rejoice in such things. Instead they were to rejoice that their names were written in heaven.

It is the same here. Those who are promised the earth, to be comforted and filled by God, to see God and be known as his children, are reminded that none of these wonderful things is as important as being deeply involved in his kingdom. This is both the beginning and the end of true discipleship.

For righteousness' sake

Jesus does not promise great rewards to the persecuted. He promises nothing to those who are persecuted because they are awkward or objectionable, or because of their imperialism or politics. He does not commend those who are fanatical or those who get in trouble because they are foolish in the way they witness to their faith.

He merely states that those who are persecuted *in the cause of righteousness* will receive his kingdom and great rewards in heaven.

To be persecuted because of righteousness is to suffer for being like Jesus. To be filled with the attitudes is to be like Jesus – and he was persecuted because of what he was like.

John 15:18–21 ☐
Luke 6:26 ☐
1 Peter 2:19–23 ☐
2 Peter 3:14–18 ☐
2 Timothy 3:12 ☐

Persecution is the inevitable consequence of being like Jesus. This is why he told his followers to pick up their crosses every day, to know that society would hate them, to be ready for suffering, disappointment and death – and to count themselves fortunate because the kingdom awaited them. We can see this in John 15:18–21; Luke 6:26; 1 Peter 2:19–23; 2 Peter 3:14–18 & 2 Timothy 3:12.

Opposition

Many believers think that the Christian faith is intrinsically attractive. They believe that their friends would soon be converted if they experienced real worship, saw an authentic miracle or met a truly Christ-like person. They miss the truth of this attitude.

Authentic Christianity has always been deeply repugnant to ordinary people. The real followers of Jesus will always be persecuted because there is something disturbingly different about Jesus and those who are ruled by him.

His teaching is unusual. His attitudes make virtues out of ideas which society despises. The lesson of history is that our unbelieving friends and relatives will not automtically embrace the genuine article when they see it. Some of them will persecute it – just as their predecessors persecuted Christ and the prophets before him.

Anyone who truly lives the first seven attitudes will experience the eighth. Like Jesus, they will find that they are not praised by the religious people of their day, they will be persecuted by them.

There is nothing that the world needs more than more people so ruled by Jesus that they have become like him. There is nothing that the church needs more than more disciples like Jesus. And only one thing is as certain that they will be persecuted because they are like him – and that is that they will receive a very great reward when the kingdom finally comes in its fullness.

While the world will persecute disciples who are like Jesus, we must remember that these followers are the ones whom God will most readily use to awaken the world to its sin and its need of the kingdom.

PART FOUR

the world and the kingdom

As disciples who have entered the kingdom and are beginning to live under the rule of God, we are caught in the tension between the 'world' and the 'kingdom'. We have to live in both at the same time.

The first section of the Sermon on the Mount after the beatitudes, Matthew 5:11–16, deals with the world's reaction to the kingdom and the kingdom's attitude to the world.

The world

The New Testament uses the word *kosmos* – world – in three ways.

1. the created world, the whole created order – John 1:10; 17:5; Romans 1:20

2. the sphere of human life – the world of humans – into which people are born – John 3:16; 6:14; 9:5, 39; 11:27; 12:19; 13:1; 14:19; 18:37; 1 Corinthians 14:10; 1 Timothy 6:7

3. the sinful world which is in conflict with God

It is this third use of *kosmos* which is meant when we consider the opposition between the kingdom and the world. In this sense, 'the world' stands for a system which is directly opposed to God, but which has more than met its match in Christ.

THE WORLD'S OPPOSITION

The New Testament paints a full and graphic picture of the tension between the world and God.

- Jesus came into the world but it knew him not – John 1:10

- apart from Jesus, the world is in spiritual darkness – John 8:12; 9:5

- the world is antagonistic to Jesus – John 7:7

- Jesus came to judge and cast out the ruler of the world – John 12:31; 14:30; 16:11, 33

- disciples are not of the world – John 17:9, 14, 16

- disciples are sent into the world to bring faith and knowledge to the world – John 17:18, 21, 23

- disciples must not love the world – 1 John 2:15, 16

- the world is passing – 1 John 2:17; 1 Corinthians 7:31

- it does not know God – 1 John 3:1

- it hates Christians – 1 John 3:13

- it receives false prophets – 1 John 4:1

- it has the spirit of the antichrist – 1 John 4:3

- it listens to its own people – 1 John 4:5

- it is in the power of the evil one – 1 John 5:19

- Jesus is the saviour of the world – 1 John 4:14

- faith in Jesus can overcome the world – 1 John 5:4–5

- the world is under the judgement of God – Romans 3:16; 1 Corinthians 6:2; 11:32

- the spirit of the world stands against the Spirit of God –
  1 Corinthians 2:12

  1 Corinthians 2:12 □

- the world is without hope and without God – Ephesians 2:12

  Ephesians 2:12 □

- Christians are lights among a perverse generation which dwells
  in the world – Philippians 2:15

  Philippians 2:15 □

- Christ has reconciled the world – 2 Corinthians 5:19

  2 Corinthians 5:19 □

- Christians live in the world without belonging to it – Colossians
  2:20

  Colossians 2:20 □

We can see that the kingdom and the world are deeply antagonistic to each other and fundamentally opposed. There can be no peaceful co-operation between them for the world opposes the righteousness of the kingdom and the kingdom exposes the sinfulness of the world. All this shows the absolute necessity for people in the world to be born again – to be changed by God from the inside. Without this work of grace, there is no hope for them.

Hatred and persecution

It is the clear testimony of the New Testament and church history that the world hates genuine Christianity and opposes it with persecution.

We must not forget this truth today, as God is increasingly blessing the church with growth. It is inevitable that the world will respond to us at some stage with the same opposition, hatred and persecution that the church has faced throughout the centuries.

- Matthew 5:11 shows that we can expected to be reviled and persecuted, and that evil will be spoken about us falsely.

  Matthew 5:11 □

- Luke 6:22 teaches that we can anticipate to be hated, excluded, reviled and cast out with an evil name.

  Luke 6:22 □

- Acts 14:22 teaches that entering the kingdom is surrounded with many tribulations.

  Acts 14:22 □

- 2 Timothy 3:12 states that *all* who desire to lead a godly life in Jesus *will* suffer persecution.

  2 Timothy 3:12 □

- 1 John 3:12–13 tells us not to be surprised if the world hates us.

  1 John 3:12–13 □

Why does the world persecute the kingdom?

The New Testament traces the opposition of the world to the kingdom from Herod's attempts to kill Jesus, through John the Baptist's imprisonment and death, Jesus' arrest and crucifixion, Peter and John's imprisonment, Stephen and James's deaths, the scattering of the believers, the widespread opposition to Paul, and the tribulation recorded in the book of Revelation.

The New Testament is more concerned to prepare disciples for persecution than to explain it. However, it seems that the world hates people who are ruled by God because their lives are radically different.

The world never accepts people who are different. Much of the worst in human behaviour is a reaction against men and women who are not the same: racism, ethnic cleansing, apartheid, class warfare, sexism, even the way people flinch when they meet a beggar or someone who is mentally handicapped.

Disciples who are filled with the attitudes of Jesus are poor in spirit, sorrowful, pure, loving, generous, merciful, hungry for righteousness, concerned with peacemaking and opposed to hypocrisy. They are against sin, selfishness and materialism. They do not put their trust in their education, their training, natural abilities or religious rituals. They are opposed to the values of the world and always stand out as different. As a result, the world responds with opposition.

Colossians 1:13 ☐

1 John 5:7 ☐

Passages like Colossians 1:13 & 1 John 5:7 emphasise the difference between people ruled by the world and those ruled by God. Images like 'light and darkness' and 'life and death' show that the world and the kingdom have nothing in common – they are totally different.

The New Testament goes further than this, though, and suggests two primary reasons why the world hates disciples.

1.   The word

John 5:24 ☐

- John 5:24 suggests that hearing the word of Jesus is linked to the transfer from death to life, from the world to the kingdom.

Matthew 13:18–23 ☐

- Matthew 13:18–23 shows that hearing the word of the kingdom is central to the struggle between the world and the kingdom. Verse 21 makes it plain that tribulation and persecution arise because of the word. Verse 22 shows that the world aims to choke the word.

- John 17:14 links Jesus' words with the world's hatred. Disciples are hated because they are 'not of the world'. And they are 'not of the world' because they have embraced Jesus' word.

John 17:14 ☐

We know that the kingdom is the personal rule of God, and we have seen that he rules us personally and directly through his word. He speaks to us and we respond to his word with belief and submission.

The world understands rules, systems, codes – legalism is at the world's heart. The kingdom, based on God's word, is anathema to the world – and the world will stop at nothing to destroy it.

2. The Christ

- John 15:18–25 shows that the world hates us because we have been chosen by Christ and belong to him. They hated him before they hated us. They hate us because Jesus has chosen us out of the world. They persecute us because they persecuted him. They oppose us for his name's sake – because of Jesus.

John 15:18–25 ☐

The persecution disciples face is not primarily personal to them. It is directed at the one who rules them. It is inflicted to hurt Christ and pain God. John 16:1–4 shows that the world does this because it knows neither God nor Jesus.

John 16:1–4 ☐

THE KINGDOM'S RESPONSE

The New Testament makes it clear that disciples who are ruled by God are called to respond to the world's opposition in three complementary ways. Each of these responses mirrors the way that Jesus dealt with the opposition he faced in his life.

1. Endure all things

In John 17:12–18, Jesus prays for his disciples. He shows that they are not of the world and that the world hates them. But instead of praying for God to remove them from the world, he asks God to protect them in the world from the evil one. Jesus sends the disciples

John 17:12–18 ☐

into the world knowing that they will face great opposition. They have to endure whatever the world will throw at them.

The endurance of the saints is stressed again and again in the New Testament. For example:

- Acts 14:22 – new disciples were exhorted to continue in the faith, and told that they entered the kingdom through many tribulations

- Romans 8:17 – our sufferings are 'with Christ'

- Romans 9:22 – endurance reveals God's power

- 1 Corinthians 4:11–16 & 2 Timothy 3:10–12 – Paul endured persecution, and urged his readers to imitate him

- Philippians 1:27–30 – we must 'stand fast' and not be terrified of our opponents

- 2 Thessalonians 1:4–8 – we must endure with patience and faith

- 2 Timothy 2:3 – we must endure as a soldier

- 2 Timothy 2:12 – our endurance will be rewarded

- Hebrews 6:15 – Abraham's patient endurance was rewarded

- Hebrews 10:29–39 – we should come alongside those enduring, and we should endure to receive something better in heaven

- James 5:11 – endurance is part of God's purpose for us

- 1 Peter 2:19–23 – endurance is commended by God

2.   Love and forgive the persecutors

In one section of the Sermon on the Mount, Matthew 5:43–48, Jesus explains how he expects his disciples to respond to enemies. If we are filled with his attitudes, we will:

- love our enemies

- bless those who curse us

- do good to those who hate us

- pray for those who persecute us

Verses 45–48 show that we are called to respond like this because this is the way that God behaves. And Luke 23:34 perfectly illustrates how Jesus responded to those who persecuted him.

Luke 23:34 ☐

Romans 12:14–21 repeats much of Jesus' teaching. We are not to be overcome by evil, rather we are to overcome evil with good – by practically caring for our enemies and blessing them.

Romans 12:14–21 ☐

3.   Rejoice when persecuted

We have already seen that, in Matthew 5:12, Jesus exhorts us to rejoice and be glad when we are persecuted. Luke 6:23 goes even further! At first sight this seems absurd. But we are not to rejoice and leap for joy because we are being persecuted, instead we are to rejoice because our reward will be great in heaven.

Matthew 5:12 ☐

Luke 6:23 ☐

- Acts 5:41; 16:25; Philippians 2:16–17 & Colossians 1:24 show how the disciples put Jesus' teaching into practice.

Acts 5:41 ☐
16:25 ☐

- Romans 5:3–5 reports how Paul gloried in tribulations because of what it produced in him.

Philippians 2:16–17 ☐

- 2 Corinthians 4:16–18 shows that the way disciples handle temporary affliction can produce 'a far more exceeding and eternal weight of glory'.

Colossians 1:24 ☐

Romans 5:3–5 ☐

- James 1:2 encourages us to rejoice at our trials because they produce patience in us.

2 Corinthians 4:16–18 ☐

- 1 Peter 4:12–19 encourages us to rejoice because we are sharing with Christ in his sufferings – and hints that there will be even greater joy at the last day.

James 1:2 ☐

1 Peter 4:12–19 ☐

LIVING THE KINGDOM IN THE WORLD

John 17:15–18 is a vital passage for understanding our kingdom relationship with the world. Jesus sends us into the world. He wants us to be deeply involved with the world. He recognises that we are not of the world and that the world hates us. Even so, rather than pray for us to be removed from the world, he prays that God will keep us safe in the world. Why does he do this? It is because he wants us to

John 17:15–18 ☐

Matthew 5:13–16 ☐

proclaim the good news to the world – by our words and our lives – so that the world can know the truth about God's love.

In Matthew 5:13–16, Jesus uses two pictures to demonstrate the way that we should be involved in a world which hates and persecutes us.

1. Salt of the earth

Matthew 5:13 states that disciples are 'the salt of the earth'. In Jesus' day, salt had five practical uses.

- it was added to food as a *flavouring* to make it more palatable

- it was rubbed into meat as a *preservative* to slow down decay

- it was thrown into human waste as a *disinfectant* to destroy germs

- it was diluted and used as an *antiseptic* to aid healing

- it was sprinkled on the soil as a *fertiliser* to increase the harvest

When Jesus states that disciples should act as salt in the world, he seems to have had all the everyday uses of salt in mind.

- The world is unpleasant – the presence of disciples ruled by God makes it less unbearable.

- The world is rotten and rotting – disciples stop it getting too dreadful.

- The world is pure garbage – disciples actively fight evil.

- The world is sick – disciples bring healing.

- The world is the soil for God's seed – disciples make the soil better prepared to receive the seed.

If we are to carry out our 'salt' function we must be deeply involved in the world. Salt cannot prevent meat from rotting unless a few grains are rubbed into the meat. It cannot bring healing unless it makes contact with disease. It cannot act as disinfectant unless it is there in the midst of the most unpleasant aspects of life. Salt cannot function as salt if it remains in a container – that is how it loses its saltiness and becomes useless – it must be 'in the world'.

Disciples act as the salt of the earth in five complementary ways:

- *our presence* – by living under God's rule, filled with the beautiful attitudes of the kingdom, our mere presence improves the world around us and makes the 'soil' more responsive to God's word.

- *our protests* – by speaking God's values, standing up for injustice, resisting what is evil, getting alongside the oppressed, our God-directed protests prevent decay, and bring healing and purification.

- *our preaching* – by announcing the good news and proclaiming God's way to life and righteousness, our words make a difference to the world as no God-inspired preaching is in vain.

- *our prayers* – by interceding for the world and on behalf of the world, our prayers engage God's power which brings change, improvement, healing and life.

- *our practical serving* – by feeding the hungry, clothing the naked, visiting the imprisoned, washing others' feet, welcoming strangers, comforting the broken-hearted, our God-guided actions change the world in the manner of salt.

Jesus' use of salt would also have had a spiritual meaning for his disciples. In the Old Testament, salt symbolises the covenant between God and his people – for example, Numbers 18:19 & 2 Chronicles 13:5. Leviticus 2:13 shows this was demonstrated by including salt in the offerings presented by the Jews – especially the grain offering.

Numbers 18:19 ☐

2 Chronicles 13:5 ☐

Leviticus 2:13 ☐

This suggests that by acting as salt in the world we evidence our covenant with God and our dependence on his sacrifice.

2. Light of the world

Matthew 5:14–16 reports Jesus' second picture of the kingdom's involvement with the world. We are the light of the world. Our light must not be hidden. Rather it must shine before men and women so that they will glorify our Father in heaven.

Matthew 5:14–16 ☐

Ephesians 4:18; 5:8–13 and Colossians 1:12–13 stress that the world is in darkness, and suggest that there is no 'grey' twilight zone. We are either light or dark. People are dark because they are controlled by the power of darkness; they become light when they are transferred to the kingdom which is ruled by 'the light of the world'.

Ephesians 4:18 ☐

5:8–13 ☐

Colossians

1:12–13 ☐

John's gospel makes much of light. His life was the light of men – 1:4. He is the real light who gives light to everyone – 1:9. He is the light of the world; anyone who follows him does not walk in the dark but has the light of life – 8:12.

Jesus' great claim to be the light of the world was made during the feast of tabernacles – 7:1–10:21. Every dusk during the feast, four golden candlesticks were lit to symbolise the pillar of fire by which God guided his people through the desert at night. Jesus' claim, set in this context, is a direct claim to divinity and permanent guidance.

John records two incidents to show the extraordinary nature of Jesus' light. An adulteress stands in the light before Jesus and is not condemned, while Pharisees walk away convicted – 8:3–12. And then, in a miracle introduced with the claim, 'I am the light of the world', a blind man sees – 9:1–7. Jesus also speaks about himself as a guiding light in John 11:10 & 12:35–36.

This suggests that God's light means guidance, miracles and compassion. In the rest of the Bible, God's light is associated with:

- *the glory of God's dwelling* – 1 Timothy 6:16

- *the nature of God* – James 1:17; 1 John 1:5

- *the favour of God* – Psalm 4:6

- *the words of God* – Psalm 119:105; Isaiah 51:4

- *the guidance of God* – Psalm 112:4; Isaiah 58:10

- *salvation* – 1 Peter 2:9

- *righteousness* – Romans 13:12; 2 Corinthians 11:14–15; 1 John 2:9–10

- *witness for God* – John 5:14–16; 5:35

Our functioning as light for the world has something to do with all these scriptural ideas. This means that, by revealing God's light, we essentially show the world what he is like.

It is important we grasp Jesus' link between light and deeds. Our light is to shine so that the world sees our *good deeds* rather than hears our *good words*. The rest of the Sermon on the Mount is essentially descriptive and illustrative of what being salt and light means in practice for those who live in the kingdom, ruled personally by God.

PART FIVE

righteousness in the kingdom

As disciples of Jesus Christ, we know that we have been called to live under the personal rule of God. This is not arbitrary, it is a rule which is always consistent with the nature of God.

We have seen how, in the Sermon on the Mount, Jesus first sets out the attitudes of the kingdom by describing the outline of the character he expects in those who follow him. We know that Jesus is more concerned with our attitudes than our actions, but that our attitudes should lead to actions which are consistent with his character.

We have also noted the conflict between the world and the kingdom, and have seen how Jesus uses the pictures of 'salt' and 'light' to describe our function in the world.

Before going on to describe God's rule in more detail, Matthew 5:17–48 contrasts the 'rule' of God with the 'rules' of God by comparing the words of Jesus with the demands of the Mosaic Law.

Matthew 5:17–48 ☐

RIGHTEOUSNESS AND THE LAW

Matthew 5:17–20 ☐

Matthew 5:17–20 is fundamental to any understanding of the relationship between disciples and the Law – the rules laid down by Moses in the Old Testament. Some teachers have used these verses to suggest that modern believers must keep some or all of the Mosaic laws, therefore we need to examine Jesus' words carefully.

- *'Do not think'* – vs. 17 shows that it is easy to misunderstand Jesus' mission. His friendship with sinners could suggest that he has low standards.

- *'The Law and the Prophets'* – vs. 17 refers to the whole of the Old Testament.

- *'I did not come to destroy but to fulfil'* – vs. 17 shows that Jesus personally came perfectly to fulfil the entire Old Testament. The Greek verb *pleroo* – 'fulfil' – means to complete. Every prophecy points to him, and he perfectly fulfils them all. Every requirement of the Law points to him, and he perfectly fulfils them.

- *'Till all is fulfilled'* – vs. 18 points to his life and death as the completion of the Law and the Prophets – it is the full stop at their end. A new era now begins, but one which is founded on the Law and the Prophets.

- *'Your righteousness must exceed the righteousness of the scribes and the Pharisees'* – vs. 20 makes it clear that Jesus had not come to lower the standards of the Law. Following him would mean living by the standards set in God's word.

When we look more widely than these verses, we can see many principles about righteousness and the Law which we need to grasp so that we can understand and appreciate the rest of Jesus' teaching in the Sermon on the Mount.

Matthew 9:9–13 ☐
12:1–14 ☐
15:1–20 ☐
4:1–11 ☐
5:17 ☐
8:4 ☐

- Jesus was not concerned to keep developments or extensions of the Law, and always stressed mercy before customs – Matthew 9:9–13; 12:1–14; 15:1–20.

- Jesus was concerned to keep the Law and to complete it – 4:1–11; 5:17; 8:4.

- Jesus' fulfilment of the Law results in a change of era. The Law and the Prophets prophesy only until John – Matthew 11:11–13. The governing principle of the Christian life is not domination by the Law. Although Christian righteousness will not simplistically continue the details of the Law, the principles behind the Law will be indirectly fulfilled and exceeded by disciples. Christian righteousness is higher than the Law as Jesus' rule is more radical.

  Matthew 11:11–13 ☐

- Becoming a disciple involves a change of kingdom. Disciples are centred on Jesus not the Law. The Law is not mentioned in any of John the Baptist's demands or in Jesus' description of life in the kingdom – Matthew 3:7–12; 5:3–16, 21–48. The rest of the Sermon focuses on living under 'God's eye'. Judgement is based on Jesus' words. The disciple's yoke is Jesus. Throughout, Jesus directly addresses the disciples and puts his personal demands on them without reference to the Law.

  Matthew 3:7–12 ☐
  5:3–16 ☐
  5:21–48 ☐

- Christian righteousness – life under Jesus, under the all-seeing 'eye of God' – is simpler than the Law, as God's rule can be summarised in a simple principle – Matthew 22:34–40.

  Matthew 22:34–40 ☐

- Christian righteousness is non legalistic for it is person-centred. It is a living relationship with Jesus. Matthew 28:18–20 shows that we are to live by his words – not by the requirements of the Old Testament law.

  Matthew 28:18–20 ☐

Matthew 5:21–48 illustrates the enormous difference between living under Jesus and living under the Law. This section of the sermon deals practically with six areas of everyday life and shows how disciples should live under God's rule.

Matthew 5:21–48 ☐

1. ANGER

In each of the six sections we will see how Jesus handles the Law, and we will compare the requirements of the Law with the rule of Jesus. The first section – 5:21–26 – deals with Exodus 20:13 which forbade murder.

Matthew 5:21–26 ☐
Exodus 20:13 ☐

First, Jesus sets out the rules with 'You have heard' and then he counters it by revealing his rule with, 'but I say to you'. This contrast, which Jesus repeats six times, can be understood in three complementary ways.

- the disciples have heard indirectly, now Jesus speaks to them directly and personally

- Moses had laid down the Law, now Jesus speaks with a higher authority

- the scribes had interpreted the Law, and added their own human traditions, now Jesus takes them back to the principles behind the Law

According to the Law, there was a wrongdoing and a punishment. 'You shall not murder, and whoever murders will be in danger of the judgement'. The judgement refers to the judicial proceedings set out in Numbers 35:12 and Deuteronomy 17:8–13.

But according to Jesus, 'Whoever is angry with his brother shall be in danger of the judgement; whoever says to his brother "Fool" shall be in danger of the council; and whoever says "Traitor" shall be in danger of hell fire'.

Jesus then goes further and shows that practical reconciliation is more important than worship. Disciples are not merely meant to be willing to be reconciled they must also take the initiative in reconciliation. This evidences the 'beautiful attitudes' of meekness and peacemaking.

Romans 12:17–18; Ephesians 4:25–32; Hebrews 12:14 & 1 John 3:15 reveal how the early church applied this area of Jesus' rule in its practical teaching.

We can see that Jesus develops the Law in four distinct ways:

1.   He makes it more radical

In the kingdom, far more is required of disciples than under the Law. Instead of merely abstaining from murder, we must also keep away from hatred and anger.

Numbers 35:12 ☐

Deuteronomy
17:8–13 ☐

Romans
12:17–18 ☐

Ephesians
4:25–32 ☐

Hebrews 12:14 ☐

1 John 3:15 ☐

2.   He makes it internal

The kingdom rule relates to words, memories and attitudes – as well as to the actual deed of murder.

3.   He increases the punishment

The judgement of the Law is dealt with in the minor courts of the country district. Jesus' judgement refers to the Great Sanhedrin, which met in Jerusalem, and then to hell fire. This shows that the issues are serious and eternal.

4.   He changes the focus

The kingdom rule is based entirely in Jesus himself. The authority and basis for the new radical requirements is totally his. He makes no reference to any authority outside of himself. It is all 'I say to you'.

In recognising how different the kingdom is from the Law, we must not forget Jesus' words that he has not come to destroy the Law. He does not give permission to murder anyone! Instead his kingdom standard is higher than the old legal standard.

2.   SEXUAL PURITY

The second section, Matthew 5:27–30, deals with another one of the 'Ten Commandments' – Exodus 20:14.

Matthew 5:27–30 ☐
Exodus 20:14 ☐

Again Jesus sets out the rules with 'You have heard' and then swiftly counters it by revealing his rule with, 'but I say to you'.

He first states the legal prohibition, 'You shall not commit adultery', and then he lays down the kingdom standard: 'Whoever looks at a woman to lust for her has already committed adultery with her in his heart.'

Jesus then goes further and shows that we must take radical, practical steps to avoid sexual sin in our thought lives as well as in our actions.

As always, Jesus' focus is more on our thoughts and attitudes than on our actions. The Law says, 'Do not do it'. The kingdom says, 'Have Jesus' mind and attitudes in you – and then you will not do it'.

1 Corinthians
    6:13–20 ☐

2 Corinthians
    6:14–7:1 ☐

2 Timothy 2:22 ☐

1 Corinthians 6:13–20; 2 Corinthians 6:14–7:1 & 2 Timothy 2:22 illustrate how this kingdom principle is developed in the early church.

We can see that Jesus develops the Law in the same distinct ways as with the previous section on murder:

1.   He makes it more radical

More is now required of disciples. Instead of merely abstaining from adultery, we must also keep away from lustful thoughts.

2.   He makes it internal

The kingdom rule relates to thoughts and attitudes towards people – as well as to the actual deed of adultery.

3.   He increases the punishment

The judgement refers to hell – again showing that eternal issues are at stake: an eternal kingdom, eternal rewards and eternal punishment.

4.   He changes the focus

The kingdom rule is again based entirely in Jesus himself. The only authority and basis for the new radical requirement is his. He still makes no reference to any authority outside of himself. He does not justify his principle by quoting anyone else. It is all his personal words to his disciples.

Once again, we must stress that Jesus does not negate or destroy the Law. He does not give us permission to commit adultery! The kingdom standard is much higher than the old legal standard – it now far exceeds that of the scribes and the Pharisees.

3. MARRIAGE

The third section, Matthew 5:31–32, contrasts the permission for divorce in the Law – Deuteronomy 24:1 – with Jesus' approach to marriage.

Matthew 5:31–32 ☐
Deuteronomy
24:1 ☐

Yet again he sets out the requirements of the Law with 'You have heard' and counters it with, 'but I say to you'.

He states the legal position and then modifies it by withdrawing the permission it gave. Rather than allowing divorce for any and every reason, Jesus stresses the permanence of marriage. In the kingdom, sexual sin is the only ground which Jesus allows for legitimate divorce.

In this section, Jesus' attitude to the Law differs from the previous two sections, as here he changes the legal requirement. It is as though Jesus considers the Old Testament rules to be inadequate for a disciple who is living under the personal rule of Jesus.

However, Jesus does not destroy the Law by making sin easier or setting a lower standard. Again, purely on his personal authority, he sets a new and higher standard. Jesus explains and develops this in Matthew 19:1–10.

Matthew 19:1–10 ☐

4. TRUTHFULNESS

The fourth section, Matthew 5:33–37, describes Jesus expressly varying another area of the Law – the rules about oaths found in Leviticus 19:12; Numbers 30:2–16 and Deuteronomy 23:22–24.

Matthew 5:33–37 ☐
Leviticus 19:12 ☐
Numbers 30:2–16 ☐
Deuteronomy
23:22–24 ☐

Once more, Jesus sets out the requirements of the Law with 'You have heard' and then counters it with, 'but I say to you'.

Jesus states the legal position, 'You shall not swear falsely, but shall perform your oaths to the Lord' and then modifies it by instructing his disciples not to make any oaths in any circumstances.

The Law demands oaths. Jesus does not prohibit false oaths or restrict the circumstances to a few serious occasions, instead he requires his followers to speak simply and straightforwardly at all times. According to Jesus, 'Anything more comes from the evil one'.

Here we see again that Jesus' rule is more radical than the Law, it is broader in its application, it is based in his personal authority, and anything contrary to his way of living comes from the enemy.

It is important we appreciate Jesus is teaching that honest disciples do not need to make oaths – he is not forbidding them from making oaths when they are required to do so. Jesus, himself, did not refuse to speak when he was put under oath in Matthew 26:63–64.

Matthew
 26:63–64 ☐

James 5:12 ☐

James 5:12 shows that the early church continued to teach disciples to live by Jesus' teaching rather than by the requirements of the Jewish law.

We should not restrict Jesus' teaching to the narrow issues of oaths. In stating that disciples should speak simply and truthfully, he is also addressing the issues of exaggeration, overstatement and understatement.

5. RIGHTS

Matthew 5:38–42 ☐

Exodus 21:24 ☐

Deuteronomy
 19:15–21 ☐

Leviticus 24:20 ☐

In the fifth section, Matthew 5:38–42, Jesus varies more of the Law – this time the rules about rights found in Exodus 21:24; Deuteronomy 19:15–21 and Leviticus 24:20.

As throughout these six sections of the Sermon on the Mount, Jesus sets out the requirements of the Law with 'You have heard' and counters it with, 'but I say to you'.

First, Jesus gives a summary of the Law, 'An eye for an eye and a tooth for a tooth'. Then he explains that the kingdom way is not to retaliate or seek revenge from those who wrong us. Disciples should not selfishly insist on retaining their rights, rather we should be generous in all our dealings with others.

The sayings in verses 39–42 are among the most radical of all Jesus' teaching – little is more contrary to the attitude and thinking of both the modern world and the Jewish law than these principles.

Romans 12:17–21 illustrates how these words of Jesus – rather than the Law – were taught in the early church.

Romans
12:17–21 ☐

6. LOVE

The last of these six contrasts between Jesus' way of righteousness and the Law – Matthew 5:43–47 – deals with love. This is his final 'You have heard that it was said, but I say to you'.

Matthew 5:43–47 ☐

Jesus is referring to Leviticus 19:18, but the second part of his quotation is not from the Law. The Law may only advocate selective love, but it does not legislate hatred. It seems reasonable to infer from this that Jesus is referring here to a first century scribal tradition which had been added to the Law.

Leviticus 19:18 ☐

Nevertheless, Jesus still sets a higher standard than the Mosaic Law by urging his disciples to love universally – even enemies. This is far beyond the requirements of the Law.

In these verses – and in Luke 6:27–36 & 10:25–37 – Jesus shows that we are called to love our enemies, to bless those who curse us, to do good to those who hate us, and to pray for those who persecute us – that we may be sons of our Father.

Luke 6:27–36 ☐
10:25–37 ☐

We do not act like this to become sons of God, we act like this because we share God's attitudes – and this is how he acts to his enemies, to those who hate and persecute him.

Finally, in Matthew 5:48, Jesus sets the standard he expects in his kingdom. We are to be perfect in the way our Father is perfect. We are to be characterised by the royal righteousness – the right being – that is appropriate to the sons and daughters of the king.

Matthew 5:21–48 ☐

Throughout this section of the Sermon on the Mount – Matthew 5:21–48 – we have seen the way that Jesus implicitly claims to have the personal right and authority to vary the Law. For example:

- in some places he intensifies the Law
- in other places he varies the Law
- he points to his authority over the Law
- he adds an internal dimension to the Law

Luke 10:27–28 ☐

Matthew 7:12 ☐

22:34–40 ☐

According to Jesus, this sort of perfect universal love is the climax of all his kingdom requirements – and is fully in keeping with the essence of the Law. We can see this very clearly in Luke 10:27–28; Matthew 7:12 and 22:34–40.

From this point on in the Sermon on the Mount, all Jesus' teaching illustrates the perfect universal love which characterises those who are ruled by him and filled with his attitudes.

PART SIX

spiritual life in the kingdom

In looking at the Sermon on the Mount, we first saw Jesus' description of the 'attitudes' he expects in disciples who are ruled by him – 5:3–12. Then, we noted the way that the world reacts to the kingdom, and the response that Jesus expects from his disciples to the world – 5:13–16. Next, we studied the relationship of the kingdom to the Law – 5:17–48. These three sections concluded in the standard Jesus set for his disciples, 'Therefore you shall be perfect, just as your Father in heaven is perfect'.

Matthew 5:3–12 ☐
5:13–16 ☐
5:17–48 ☐

This is now followed by a new section where Jesus offers a picture of disciples living in the world under 'the eye of God' – in total submission to God and in entire dependence on him.

In Matthew 5, Jesus outlined the character of disciples, described how we should behave in society, and showed us the standards he expects us to live by.

Now, in Matthew 6, he offers a picture of disciples living that kingdom life in the world. He constantly emphasises that we live in the world in the presence of the all-seeing God. The dominant theme

Matthew 6:1–18 ☐
6:19–34 ☐

of this chapter is the disciples' relationship with their Father as they live under the rule of God in the world.

Chapter six considers two areas of our lives. Firstly, in verses 1–18 it deals with our spiritual lives; and secondly, in verses 19–34, it focuses on our ordinary 'everyday' lives. The kingdom is not concerned with only one or two areas of our lives – God wants to rule in *every* aspect of our living.

PRINCIPLES OF KINGDOM SPIRITUALITY

Living in the kingdom means that our lives are constantly open and exposed before the king. As we live in the presence of God, we can have no secrets from him and should be real in our relationship with him.

Matthew 6:1 ☐
5:16 ☐

Matthew 6:1 introduces Jesus' teaching about our spiritual lives, and lays down the general principles which govern the spiritual side of kingdom living: 'Take heed that you do not do your acts of righteousness before men, to be seen by them. Otherwise you have no reward from your Father in heaven.'

Godly balance

At first sight, this verse seems to contradict Jesus' instruction in 5:16. There he commands that our light – our good deeds – should shine before men. Yet here Jesus says that our acts of righteousness should not be done before men. But if everything is to be done in secret, behind a closed door, how can people see the light?

Jesus' first saying states that we shine before men 'so that they may glorify your Father in heaven'. His second saying insists that we must not do acts of righteousness before men 'to be seen by them'.

There is no contradiction here, it is merely that the motivation is expressed differently. Disciples are called to live in such a way that, when people look at us, they see and glorify God. We must not do anything to attract attention to ourselves. We must not want to be noticed – rather we should be characterised by the self-effacing humility of the Holy Spirit.

We all face two opposite temptations: either to be too ostentatious in our lives or to be too reclusive. Some Christians make far too much of a show of everything they do, whereas others are so terrified of self that they hide away from the world. We need a godly balance between these extremes.

If we approach Christ's teaching here as 'yet more rules' from God we are bound to go wrong. But if we grasp the principle that he is setting out – and live by his personal rule – we will steer clear of hypocrisy.

In some wonderful way, we are called to attract attention towards us so that people glorify *God*, yet we must not attract any attention towards us so that people focus on *us*.

Pleasing God

Superficially, verse 1 seems to pose a choice between pleasing people and pleasing God. But most of us only really try to please others because we want to please ourselves. We want to please them and impress them so that they will think more highly of us!

This can mean that an action which appears to be godly can actually be sinful because of its self-centred motivation. Men and women naturally want more to be praised and rewarded by people than by God. However, Jesus says his disciples should act in such a way that our sole aim is to please God.

God sees everything

Our chief object in life should be to please God, to please only God, and to please him in everything. When this is our aim, we really will be starting to live under the rule of God.

We follow Jesus who lived exactly like this. He lived entirely for God. His words and deeds were his Father's. He never put his own needs or will first. Mark 7:24, 31–37; 8:22–26 show his desire to work unobtrusively. He was not concerned with what people thought about him, for he lived only for the glory of God.

Mark 7:24 ☐
7:31–37 ☐
8:22–26 ☐

Matthew 6:1 ☐

If our absolute priority is to live and work for God only under his rule – and we are not over-concerned what other people think – we will find it easier to live by Jesus' principle in Matthew 6:1.

It follows on from this that disciples who are under 'God's rule' are also under 'God's eye'. He sees all our thoughts and actions. There is nothing we can think or do which is missed by him. There is nowhere we can go to escape from his sight. We are always in his presence. He is always 'God with us'. Our lives will be revolutionised when we really grasp this wonderful – and rather frightening – truth.

There is so much pretence and sham in the way that we present ourselves to other people – yet God is watching and recording it all. Everything in this section of the Sermon on the Mount is based on this principle. Again and again, Jesus reminds us that our God is the 'Father who sees in secret'.

Holy rewards

If we do the right thing for the right reason, we will be rewarded by God. This is a basic kingdom principle which we already noted many times. When we please God, he promises to reward us. When we do not please him, he promises to judge us in some way.

Hebrews 12:2 ☐
11:23–26 ☐

Hebrews 12:2 shows that Jesus endured the cross and despised the shame because of the joy which was set before him. And Hebrews 11:23–26 points out that Moses was motivated in part by the reward which was before him.

2 Corinthians 5:9–10 ☐

The New Testament teaches so much about the differing rewards which God will distribute to disciples that we should not be embarrassed by looking and working for them. 2 Corinthians 5:9–10 is a critical passage on this topic.

We must recognise Jesus' stress that God will not reward those who have sought some reward from people. This is an absolute statement without any qualifications.

If we are concerned with what people think about our worshipping, we will get nothing from God. If we are hoping for human appreciation for our acts of service or duty, we will receive nothing from God. If we seek any notice or reward or thanks or commendation from people, that is all we will get.

Having set out his general principles of the kingdom in Matthew 6:1, Jesus illustrates this in three areas of our spiritual lives – giving, praying and fasting. In each area he contrasts a wrong and a right way of worshipping God.

- We are not to worship like hypocrites – in a way designed to attract people's attention.

- We will have no reward if we worship like a hypocrite.

- We are to worship discreetly – without any show.

- We are to worship remembering that God is watching.

- We will be rewarded by God if we worship in his way.

GIVING GOD'S WAY

Giving is Jesus' first example of kingdom spirituality. In Matthew 6:2–4, he shows disciples how they should be real in their giving. Jesus uses the Greek word *eleemosune* which means 'an act of mercy'. Jesus is not talking about giving money, instead he is speaking about helping people in the widest possible way. This involves giving money, time, attention – any kind deeds.

Matthew 6:2–4 ☐

Do not announce it to others

The wrong way of giving is to announce it to other people. Jesus paints a ridiculous picture of people engaging a trumpeter to go in front of them to announce, 'Look what this person has done'.

Of course, very few people do this so blatantly. Most of us are much more subtle about letting people know what we have done. But our 'sharing for prayer or praise' can be our modern-day version of a first-century trumpet!

Jesus' kingdom rule is simply 'no announcing to others'. If we do this, we have had all the reward that we are going to get.

Do not announce it to yourself

Jesus' right way of giving involves a second negative, 'Do not let your left hand know what your right hand is doing, that your charitable deed may be in secret'.

This shows that we are not even to announce our giving to ourselves. This means not making note of our actions, not storing them up in our memory, not keeping some sort of internal account of what we have done for others and God.

We are simply to do as we are moved and led by God – and then to forget about it. We are to have such a love for God and others that we do not have time to think about ourselves. This is a practical way of expressing our poverty of spirit, meekness and death to self.

Matthew
25:31–40 ☐
In Matthew 25:31–40, the righteous are puzzled by the King's words. 'Lord, when did we see you hungry and feed you, or thirsty and give you drink? When did we see you a stranger and take you in, or naked and clothe you? Or when did we see you sick, or in prison, and come to you?'

This illustrates how the righteous are meant to be unaware of what they have done. They have not kept a record of their giving. But the Father who sees in secret notes, remembers – and rewards.

PRAYING GOD'S WAY

Matthew 6:5–15 ☐
Jesus' second example of kingdom spirituality is prayer. In Matthew 6:5–15 he shows disciples how they should be real in their praying. Jesus uses the commonest Greek word for prayer *proseuchomai* to show that he is talking about prayer in the widest possible sense.

Do not show off in praying

Again, Jesus shows a right and a wrong way of worshipping God. The wrong way of praying focuses attention on the one who is praying rather than on the One to whom prayer is offered.

Jesus paints a picture of people who pray in a way which gets them known as people who pray. As with giving, some people do it in an obvious way whereas most of us are more subtle. Too many disciples say and do things which ensure that other people are impressed with them because of their praying.

Jesus does not say that this negates our praying. He does not say that God will not hear or answer our prayers. He simply states that human adulation or approval is all the reward we are going to have. We will miss out on a reward in heaven.

Do not have a set formula for prayer

Jesus also instructs us not to use 'vain repetitions' when we pray. This does not refer only to those who say the same prayer again and again and again. Many of us have a routine in prayer which we rigidly follow – and this can mean that we forget what and why we are doing it.

Prayer is communion with God. It is conversation with the Father. If we pay too much attention to the form of words we use we can lose the spontaneity of the intimate relationship of true prayer.

God does not want us to measure our praying by the amount of time we spend in prayer, or by the form of words we use. If we value a type of praying, or a form of words, or a way of praying, or a length of praying – we will lose our heavenly reward.

But if we pray in God's discreet way, not only will our prayers be answered, we will also be openly rewarded by the Father.

Focus on approaching God

Jesus' right way of worshipping God in prayer begins with the realisation that we are approaching God. When this thought is uppermost, everything else falls into place.

In verse 6, Jesus shows that we focus on God by excluding everything else. We are not meant literally to sit in a cupboard to pray – this is an illustration of shutting out thoughts about other people, and shutting out thoughts about ourselves, so that we can concentrate totally on our communion with God.

When we concentrate on God, we know that we can approach him confidently claiming all the biblical promises about prayer. The *Sword of the Spirit* book *'Effective Prayer'* offers a full biblical picture of approaching God in prayer and the different types of prayer.

Follow Jesus' pattern

In verses 9–13, Jesus gives a framework for all praying rather than a set prayer to be prayed over and over again. As he has told us not to repeat ourselves endlessly, it is rather strange that some believers do exactly that with this prayer!

Jesus does not want us to pray in the hypocritical manner he describes in verses 5–7. He does not want us to pray just to make an impression on others. He does not want us to pray publicly at enormous length. He also explains that God already knows all our needs and, therefore, he does not need to be educated about our circumstances.

Instead, Jesus tells us to pray 'in this manner'. The Lord's Prayer is his example prayer. 'Pray like this' he says, and offers us a 'prayer skeleton' for us to flesh out. As we pray, we fill in the specific details which are relevant to our situation.

- *'Our Father'*

The prayer is both personal and corporate. This is a personal prayer which can be prayed privately – yet it uses 'we' and 'our' throughout. This suggests that we should unite ourselves with each other whenever we pray.

This phrase teaches that, when we pray, we should remind ourselves both about the relationship we have with God through faith in Christ *and* the fellowship we share with others. In prayer, we should tell God what his fatherhood means to us – and thank him for it.

- *'in heaven'*

Our prayers should be governed by the realisation that God is the king and is in total control. We can ask him to help us to become more aware of his greatness and presence.

- *'hallowed be your name'*

This phrase reminds us to pray as Jesus does in John 17 – to ask for God's glory and the holiness of his name to be recognised and experienced in specific ways. God is a good Father who delights to give us good things and he reveals different aspects of his nature through his varied names.

When we pray, it is helpful to address God by whichever of his names is most appropriate to our prayer – for example, Healer, Provider, Deliverer, Guide, Creator, Saviour, Shepherd, and so on.

- *'your kingdom come'*

This helps us to remember to pray that God will establish his rule by extending his influence as people bow their knees to Jesus Christ, and as we submit increasingly to Christ's reign. Asking for God's kingdom to come means asking him to rule – to have his way – in the situations and lives for which we are praying.

- *'your will be done on earth as it is in heaven'*

The coming of God's kingdom means that the conditions of heaven are revealed on earth. Of course, this will not take place fully until the kingdom comes in its final manifestation, but – in the meantime – we should pray for God's revealed will to be done in those specific situations on earth which concern us.

We can thank God that he wants his will to be done on earth, and we can have faith that this will happen as we pray.

- *'give us this day our daily bread'*

This shows that we should pray for the physical needs of daily life. It is God's intention that all his children should receive what they need, but we must take whatever action is necessary to provide for ourselves.

We should pray especially for needs which we ourselves are helpless to meet. We experience the truth of God's provision only through a combination of prayer and action.

- *'and forgive us our debts'*

We need to pray for spiritual forgiveness from our heavenly Father *and* for financial forgiveness from merciless or unjust human creditors. The judicial forgiveness we have as redeemed believers is already ours, but we need daily cleansing to maintain our personal communion with God.

As with daily bread, forgiveness from debts is attained by a mixture of prayer and action. We should pray either for the needs which we cannot meet ourselves, or that God will enable us personally to meet the needs through the resources he has given us.

- *'as we forgive our debtors'*

Jesus makes it plain that our heavenly Father will withhold his parental forgiveness from us if we withhold our forgiveness from others.

- *'and do not lead us into temptation'*

This phrase shows that we should ask God to keep us from falling into sin and to help us overcome the trials of our lives.

- *'but deliver us from the evil one'*

When most people recite the Lord's Prayer, they unwittingly use a translation called 'The Great Bible' which is even older than the Authorised Version. It refers unhelpfully to 'evil' rather than to 'the evil one'.

We are all involved in a spiritual struggle, and we all need to pray that God will rescue us from the attacks of the enemy.

- *'for yours is the kingdom and the power and the glory for ever. Amen.'*

Jesus' model prayer ends in a phrase packed with praise and triumph taken from 1 Chronicles 29:11–12. We can end our praying by thanking God for his power – and for his victory in the specific situations that we have prayed about.

1 Chronicles
29:11–12 ☐

FASTING GOD'S WAY

Jesus' third example of kingdom spirituality is fasting. In Matthew 6:16–18, he shows his disciples how they should be real in their fasting.

Matthew 6:16–18 ☐

His first example examined the way we do good to other people. His second focused on our communion with God. These verses look at the way we discipline ourselves in our spiritual lives. Although Jesus' words are especially about fasting – going without food to intensify our praying – they are also relevant to the more general way that we treat ourselves.

Under Old Testament law, there was only one compulsory fast which took place every year on the Day of Atonement. We can read about this in Leviticus 16:29–34 & 23:27–32. Zechariah 8:19 shows that, after the Jews returned from exile, four other compulsory fasts were observed as well.

Leviticus
    16:29–34 ☐
    23:27–32 ☐
Zechariah 8:19 ☐

We know that Jesus fulfilled or completed the entire Old Testament – both the Law and the Prophets. This means that there is now no legal reason for fasting. But this does not mean that we must not fast. Rather, it means that we do not have to fast either to be righteous or as a legalistic duty. Jesus does not condemn fasting in these verses, he merely condemns fasting with wrong motives.

Do not fast for self-mortification

Fasting has no value as a means of dealing with the pull towards sin in our lives. It does not make us holy. The flesh is dealt with only in the power of the Spirit as we put to death those deeds of the flesh which are associated with old, non-Christian ways of living.

In fact, this motive for fasting indulges ourselves as it delights in the showy and external forms of so-called spirituality which Jesus condemns.

Do not fast for self-merit

It is foolish to think that by fasting, or any other act, we win God's favour, receive his grace, or force him to bless us or answer our prayers. God's grace is freely given. He answers our prayers only through Jesus Christ and because of his finished work on the cross.

Do not fast for self-assertion

The Pharisees had an ostentatious approach to fasting – as they did to every spiritual practice. They drew attention to their twice-weekly fasting in quite a forceful way. They were spiritual show-offs. Jesus condemns this and speaks of the rewards of fasting as coming only to those whose motives are right. If we draw attention to our fasting in any way we will lose our heavenly reward.

Fast to express sorrow for sin

2 Samuel 1:11–12 ☐

2 Samuel 1:11–12 shows how fasting expresses grief and mourning. Fasting can be a natural human reaction, but it can also go beyond that and become a way of coming before God and expressing our deep concern and sorrow over a range of things – as in Nehemiah 1:4. Fasting in this way is legitimate, and through it we can experience the blessing of Matthew 5:4.

Nehemiah 1:4 ☐

Matthew 5:4 ☐

We can react in the same way over any serious situation – to do with the nation, the state of the Church, or some personal matter which confronts us. In the Bible, fasting of this kind is often linked with mourning for sin and humbling oneself before God and his mercy. Fasting is not 'doing penance' for sin, but it does come out of a personal understanding of the seriousness of sin.

Fast to express seriousness with God

Throughout the Bible, fasting is linked to prayer. It is not enough merely to fast. The whole purpose of fasting is to create more time to pray and to show a seriousness of purpose in prayer.

When we fast, we say to God, 'Lord, this situation, that has brought me to my knees before you, is of more concern to me than my normal bodily needs of food and nourishment.'

Fasting is powerful because we come to God at a deeper level of seriousness. It is this determination that God honours, and in fasting it takes on a new dimension. Isaiah 58 talks of spiritual, and not merely physical or social bonds being broken through fasting by the power of the Holy Spirit.

Fast for the reward

Jesus promised that the Father would reward sincere and single-minded seeking after him. Matthew 6:18 shows that this includes fasting in God's way.

Matthew 6:18 ☐

There is something powerful about fasting which, if done with a pure heart and godly motives, brings us closer to God. James 4:10 and Isaiah 40:31 illustrate this principle.

James 4:10 ☐

Isaiah 40:31 ☐

If our main concern is to please God and glorify him, we will not have any difficulty with the idea of fasting. We will not worry what other people think about us – so we will not feel the need to act like the hypocrites in verse 16 and dress or act to impress others by our spirituality.

When we live under the rule of God, we do not need rules which tell us when to fast, what to wear, how to pray, and so on. God himself will speak directly to us and guide all our being and doing.

When we are completely pre-occupied with God – concerned only to be right before him and to please him in everything – we will know that we are safe in his hands. And he who sees all the secrets of our spiritual lives will reward us openly at the great day which is coming.

PART SEVEN

physical life in the kingdom

In Matthew 5, Jesus outlines the character of true disciples, describes how they should behave in society, and sets out the standards he expects them to live by. In Matthew 6, he offers a picture of living his kingdom life in the world; and we have noted that the dominant theme of this chapter is our relationship with the Father – as we live under the rule of God in the world.

Chapter six considers two areas of a disciple's life. In Part Six we looked at the way verses 1–18 deal with the spiritual dimension of our lives. Now we move on to examine what verses 19–34 teach about the ordinary, 'everyday' physical part of our lives.

Matthew 6:19–34 □

The basic questions we need to go on asking ourselves about our spiritual life are, 'Who am I trying to please or impress?' and, 'What is my motive?' The key fact we need always to remember is that the all-seeing God is watching us – he sees what we do and think in secret.

Verses 19–34 suggest that the basic questions we must answer about our physical life are, 'Who is my master?' and 'Who am I serving?' The important fact we need continually to recall is that God will tolerate no rival powers in the lives of his subjects.

These verses show that God is looking for total loyalty and absolute trust in those who are living in his kingdom. These are the issues of lordship/kingship/government which are fundamental to discipleship.

Jesus deals with two problems or temptations.

* verses 19–24 show that we must not *serve* or love the world

* verses 25–34 say that we must not *worry* about the world

It is important we see that Jesus treats both aspects of the problem in terms of our relationship with the Father.

GOD OR MAMMON?

Matthew 6:24 ☐

Matthew 6:24 states that disciples 'cannot serve God and *mammon*'. *Mammon* is the Aramaic word for wealth or riches, and Jesus' use of it here suggests that 'wealth' is a rival to God for our affections. *Mammon* is a power which attempts to dominate and enslave us – when we should be ruled only by God.

This does not mean that coins and notes are evil, rather that there are spiritual forces behind the material form of wealth. These forces promise us access to power, position, prestige, privilege and protection – through wealth or riches. These dark forces have a power which grips most people's lives, but which should have no hold on disciples.

According to Jesus, the power of money is a false-God from which we must turn to serve the true and living God. The on-going rejection of *mammon* in our physical lives is a basic requirement of discipleship.

Wealth can make people feel secure. It seems to offer freedom, power and contentment. People everywhere seek it furiously. Yet God wants his disciples to find their security, freedom, power and contentment in Christ alone – and to seek him and his heavenly treasure with everything that they have.

In verses 19–21, Jesus contrasts storing treasures for ourselves on earth and in heaven. He shows that earthly treasure can be spoilt and stolen, whereas heavenly treasure is permanent. Jesus' wider teaching about wealth and money helps us to see how we can seek the best treasure and resist the power of *mammon*.

Demands of discipleship

We have already seen that, time and again, Jesus asked people to leave all and follow him. Forsaking *mammon* is part of turning from everything to follow Christ, part of being a disciple of Christ, and part of ministering with Christ. For example:

- Levi left the world of *mammon* to become a disciple – Luke 5:27–28.

  Luke 5:27–28 ☐

- Simon, Andrew, James & John left their business and their wonderful catch to be disciples – Luke 5:1–11.

  Luke 5:1–11 ☐

- The law-keeping, rich young ruler found the pull of *mammon* more attractive than the promise of heavenly inheritance – Luke 18:18–23.

  Luke 18:18–23 ☐

- The twelve's ministry instructions left no room for *mammon* – Matthew 10:7–10.

  Matthew 10:7–10 ☐

- The seventy two were given similar orders – Luke 10:1–12.

  Luke 10:1–12 ☐

Heavenly and earthly treasure

In Matthew 6:19–21, Jesus gives disciples a straightforward choice: earthly or heavenly treasure. In 6:24, he explains that 'no one can serve two masters; for either he will hate the one and love the other, or else be loyal to the one and despise the other. You cannot serve God and *mammon*.'

Matthew 6:19–24 ☐

It is obviously sensible for disciples to choose heavenly treasure, yet the power of *mammon* makes it difficult for us to resist the temptation to hunger after earthly treasures.

In Luke 12:33–34, Jesus explains how we store up or earn heavenly treasure. It is clear that the generous actions which he describes also destroy the power of *mammon* in our lives.

Luke 12:33–34 ☐

Luke 16 is an important chapter about *mammon* and true riches. Instead of being enslaved by *mammon*, we are called to use wealth in such a way that we enter into 'eternal habitations' and 'true riches'.

Matthew 5:42 ☐

Luke 6:30–38 ☐

Disciples who submit to the rule of God have been released from their slavery to *mammon*. They are called to evidence this both by faithful stewardship and by giving with God's generosity and compassion. Jesus urges us to give like God in verses like Matthew 5:42 & Luke 6:30–38 – these passages outline the actions which God rewards with heavenly treasure.

Good and bad eyes

Matthew 6:19–24 ☐

At first sight, verses 22–23 seem to interrupt Jesus' teaching. Superficially, verse 24 appears to be in the wrong place; it seems that it should follow directly on from 19–21. Yet we know that this cannot be right thinking.

Verse 24 comes after verses 22–23 – as well as after 19–21 – because Jesus' conclusion 'You cannot serve God and *mammon*' has as much to do with these two verses as with the preceding two.

Verses 19–21 focus on 'storing' *mammon*, on having our hearts set on amassing wealth and material 'possessions', on the attitude which says 'these are mine, I can do with them what I want'. Verses 22–23 deal with 'seeing' *mammon*, with constantly seeing things that we want or think that we need, with minds which are so full of the things of *mammon* that there is little space left for the things of God.

We serve *mammon* not just be putting our trust in wealth and hanging on to what we have, but also by constantly thinking about material things – by seeing them in our 'mind's eye', by daydreaming about how our life would improve if only we had this or that.

These verses are Jesus' way of describing how we look at things. According to him, there are only two ways of looking at everything in the world.

- *the good eye* – this is the disciple's eye which sees things God's way, which sees everything as it truly is without any 'double vision'

- *the bad eye* – this is the eye which sees thing blurred and out of focus, coloured by prejudices and worldly desires

In verse 21, Jesus stated that our heart is where our treasure is. Now he shows that our minds are also affected by the treasure offered by *mammon*. Our views and ethical outlook are often tainted by a way of thinking which places a false value on material things. This is a way which turns to *mammon* rather than to God for security and hope.

Paul's comments about a colleague, in 2 Timothy 4:10, show how much these things can affect our service. Sadly, many disciples do not recognise this – their eyes are not sharp and clear.

2 Timothy 4:10 ☐

In Luke 21:34–36, Jesus warns his disciples that the ordinary cares of the world are just as dangerous as drunkenness in distracting them from following him as closely as they should.

Luke 21:34–36 ☐

Earthly treasures are so powerful that they grip the entire human personality. The enemy uses them to tear at our hearts, our minds and our wills. We have established that what we do is the result of what we think – now we can see that what we think is determined by our treasure. Whatever aspect of life we examine, the same principle is always true. Our treasure – what we value most highly of all – will determine the way that we think and act.

Loving and hating God

Matthew 6:24 is one of Jesus' most serious statements: 'No one can serve two masters; for either he will hate the one and love the other, or else he will be loyal to the one and despise the other. You cannot serve God and *mammon*'.

Both God and *mammon* – the love of earthly treasures – make absolute demands on us. Worldly, physical things demand our entire devotion. They want us to prize them above all else and to live for them. So does God.

Jesus' words in Luke 18:22 and Matthew 10:37 illustrate the total demands of the kingdom. We are called to be ruled only by God – there is not meant to be any room in our affections for a rival. It is 'either/or'. Compromise is impossible.

Luke 18:22 ☐

Matthew 10:37 ☐

Many disciples do not realise that all materialism is against God. They recognise that some economic systems which are openly anti-God are incompatible with Christianity, but they have not grasped the biblical truth that every form of materialism is essentially atheistic.

According to Jesus, if we have some love for material things we actually hate God. There are many, many people who think that they are Christian people – they worship, pray, read the Bible, witness, and so on. But they are also living for earthly treasures. Verse 23 comments, 'How great is that darkness!'

2 Kings 17:24–41 □

The story, in 2 Kings 17:24–41, of the Assyrians is a striking parallel of many modern disciples. They genuinely feared the true God – but they continued to serve their own gods as well. They tried to mix following God with following their old pagan ways – 'even to this day'.

Matthew 7:21–23 □
6:24 □

We should not be surprised when we reach Jesus' conclusion to the Sermon on the Mount in Matthew 7:21–23. It is a natural conclusion to his words in 6:24. We either serve God or *mammon*. It is all God and no *mammon* – or some *mammon* and no God.

For many believers, the vitality of their spiritual lives is the measure of their devotion to God. Yet it seems that Jesus is even more concerned with the physical dimension of our lives. We can pray, fast and help people and still be fascinated by *mammon* and earthly treasure. But we will always put God and his rule first when we have no time for the things of *mammon*.

WORRY OR FAITH?

Matthew 6:25–34 □

In Matthew 6:19–24, Jesus stresses the danger of storing treasures on earth, of living to any degree for material possessions. In verses 25–34, he goes on to emphasise the pointlessness of worrying about these sorts of earthly things.

Some disciples may not have much wealth or many possessions, but they can still be in the grip of *mammon* because they are always worrying about the physical problems of life.

The enemy does not mind whether we store wealth or worry about it. All he is concerned about is ensuring that our minds are on *mammon* rather than on God. His one concern is to distract disciples from focusing on God – and he will use any means to achieve this aim.

In these verses, Jesus reasons with his disciples. He uses three arguments, and introduces each one with the same phrase, 'Therefore do not worry' – verses 25, 31 & 34.

Do not be distracted

Most versions of the Bible translate the Greek verb *merimnao* slightly differently. They use expressions like 'take no thought', 'be not anxious' and 'do not worry'. However, *merimnao* is derived from *merizo* – which means to divide something with another, or to share with. *Merimnao* literally means 'to divide the mind'.

Jesus is telling his disciples that they must not have a mind which is divided into sections, which is torn between two ideas, which thinks one thought today and another thing tomorrow, which is not focused entirely on God. He is urging us 'do not be distracted' from God and his rule and his reliable character.

Luke 10:38–42 illustrates this with its comment that Martha was 'distracted'. Jesus told her that she was worried and troubled about many things, but that her sister had one purpose – to hear Jesus' words. | Luke 10:38–42 ☐

In Matthew 6:25–34, Jesus is warning us not to be distracted from the main objective of a disciple with worries about the ordinary physical matters of life. He is not saying that we must *never* think about food and clothes and health; rather he is urging us not to allow these things to distract us from focusing on God's word.

In his first 'Do not worry' – verses 25–30 – Jesus gives four reasons why disciples must not be double-minded or distracted.

1.   There is more to life

Firstly, he reminds us that our life is much more important than the food we eat and the clothes we wear. These are peripheral matters which should not burden us with worry and anxiety. Other things are far more important.

We need to remember that God has given us our lives. He is the ultimate source behind everything we have and are. He is the ultimate provider behind our daily requirements of food, clothing and health. And, because he made us and sustains us, we need not worry that we will have less than enough.

Like the birds, we have to find our food and build our nests. But, like the birds, God will see that we have what we need. Jesus does not explain how God provides, he simply points out that God does provide.

2. God is our heavenly Father

Jesus points out, in verse 26, that God provides for all his creation – and we are part of that. But he then reminds his disciples that the Creator is also their 'heavenly Father'.

We do not need to worry because God provides for all his creatures. But disciples are not just God's creatures, we are also in a personal relationship with him – we are his children and he is our Father. Therefore we have even less justification for our worry. If God cares for his animals, do we really dare think that he will forget about his children?

3. Worry is futile

In verse 27, Jesus reminds his disciples about the essential pointlessness of worry. It is impotent. Worry can accomplish nothing – it is a complete waste of time.

Nobody knows whether Jesus means increasing the length of our life or the height of our body, but worry changes neither of these things. Our life is a gift from God. He starts it, he ends it, he sustains it – we are in completely in his hands. Our Father is behind everything, therefore we need not, and should not, waste time with futile worry.

4. Worry shows little faith

In verse 30, Jesus states that disciples who worry about the physical things of life demonstrate that they have little faith. This is their problem, the real cause of all their worrying.

Jesus does not accuse these disciples of having no faith – for they are his disciples and they are listening to his words. They believe in Jesus enough to have started to follow him, but they do not believe him enough not to worry.

Many disciples are sure that God has done everything to give them salvation in the life to come, but they are far from convinced that God will look after them in this life on earth. They have a spiritual faith but not a physical faith. They have divided their lives into sections, and they trust God to look after their spiritual dimension but not their physical needs.

After giving these four reasons why disciples should not worry about physical needs, Jesus moves on – in verses 31–34 – to his second 'Do not be distracted' and offers three important conclusions.

1.   Be different from the pagans

Right through the Sermon on the Mount, Jesus constantly emphasises that the kingdom is opposed to the world and that the attitudes of the kingdom are not those of the world. He returns to this theme in verse 32 and shows that disciples are meant to seek after quite different things from the people around them.

Our friends and neighbours worry about physical matters like money, work, housing, holidays, car, food and clothes. We should stand out as different – in both our thinking and our speaking. The whole theme of the sermon is that kingdom living is utterly different from worldly living, and this is just another illustration of Jesus' main point.

2.   Know that God knows

Again and again in the sermon, Jesus keeps on gently reminding his disciples that their Father sees and knows. He knows what we think; he sees what we do; he is aware of our every need. It should be a wonderful relief for us that God does know all our deepest needs – nothing is hidden from him. Disciples who really grasp this truth are those who become free from worry and anxiety.

3.   Concentrate on the kingdom

Matthew 6:33 is one of the most well-known verses in the Bible: 'But seek first the kingdom of God and his righteousness, and all these things shall be added to you'.

Matthew 6:33 ☐

Instead of worrying about the physical matters of life, disciples should concentrate on their relationship with God – on being ruled personally and directly by him, and on his 'right being'.

This is not a verse for unbelievers about becoming a Christian, it is a verse for disciples about being a Christian. We are to put the kingdom first. We are to seek God's rule with every fibre of our being. We are to think more about our relationship with God than anything else.

We saw in the attitudes that it is the disciples who are hungry and thirsty for righteousness who are filled. It is the same principle here. The disciples who seek first the kingdom and God's righteousness are the ones who discover – almost by accident – that they also have everything else they need for their earthly life in the world.

The world seeks worldly things, and finds worry, anxiety, fear. But disciples who seek God find peace, certainty, security – plus adequate physical provision.

Faith for the future

Matthew 6:34 □

Matthew 6:34 contains Jesus' final 'Do not be distracted'. Here he takes his teaching about worry a further step and deals with anxiety about the future. If the enemy cannot tempt us to worry about the physical problems which face us today, he will try to overwhelm us with fear for the future.

Many disciples trust God for today, but seem unconvinced that he can help them tomorrow. They envisage all sorts of possibilities and unlikely scenarios – and worry about them all! They are always asking themselves 'What if this happens?', 'What about this possibility?', 'How will I manage?'

Everything Jesus has said in this section about worry and faith applies to the future as well. Worry is futile. The Father knows what we will need. We must have faith; be different; seek the kingdom – and so on.

When we worry about the future, we cripple ourselves for today. Because we live in a fallen world, a world opposed to the kingdom, almost every day has some degree of hardship or difficulty. We need to go on seeking God for his direction and strength to deal with everything that the world is throwing at us today. And we need to ensure that we are not distracted by anything in the future – especially by worrying about things which may not happen or which God will deal with at the right time.

We need to resist and refuse the thoughts which tempt us to worry about the future. Instead, we should seek God's kingdom and his right way of being for today – knowing that the God we rely on today will be just as reliable tomorrow.

PART EIGHT

judgement in the kingdom

We have seen that the Sermon on the Mount began with Jesus' description of a disciple's character. It continued through Matthew 5 by outlining a disciple's relationship to the world and to the Law, and through chapter six by examining a disciple's life in the world in relationship with the Father. Now, in Matthew 7:1–6, the sermon moves on to Jesus' description of his disciples' relationships with other people.

Matthew 7:1–6 ☐

DO NOT JUDGE

Judgement is the great theme which runs throughout all of chapter seven. Jesus begins this section with a clear and simple statement, 'Judge not', which he follows with three reasons why disciples should not judge others.

This principle cannot mean that disciples must never make any judgements or express any opinions, for verse 6 would be impossible to apply if disciples could never make any form of judgement – we cannot identify a 'dog' or a 'pig' without exercising some form of judgement. Verse 15 would be equally difficult to understand, for there Jesus sets out the principles involved in judging whether someone is a false prophet or not.

Jesus is not telling us never to exercise judgement, rather he is concerned with the way that we criticise and condemn others. Jesus is forbidding the wrong kind of judging. He is warning us against the critical attitude which condemns other people, which feels superior and self-righteous, which regards others with contempt. This is the attitude which delights to criticise, which approaches everything expecting to find fault, which seems almost to hope for the worst.

Throughout the sermon, Jesus is always more concerned with our attitudes than our actions. It is the same here: it is crucial that disciples have a godly manner and Christ-like motives when they judge others and offer opinions.

We can say that judging is wrong when it:

- **is done in a negative and critical way** – Any criticism is sinful if the motive is to tear down and not to build up, even though the criticism may, in itself, be accurate.

- **is done in a spirit of self-righteousness** – People often criticise others to direct attention away from themselves, to appear free from fault, or to shift the blame onto another. We see this in Genesis 3:12.

Genesis 3:12 ☐

- **is not softened by mercy** – We know that disciples are called to be merciful, so judgement should never be made in a harsh or unforgiving way. We should always be positive and generous in the way we talk about and evaluate others. We see this in Ephesians 4:2, 32 & Philippians 4:5.

Ephesians 4:2, 32 ☐

Philippians 4:5 ☐

- **is made in a biased or prejudiced way** – People are often more generous in their evaluation of themselves and the people they like than of those they dislike. Judgement is wrong if it comes from a background of prejudice against the person, or the class or group that the person comes from – James 2:1–4.

James 2:1–4 ☐

- **is given without all the facts** – A partial presentation of truth usually conveys a completely false picture. A selective use of facts is likely to lead to a wrong judgement – Proverbs 18:17.

Proverbs 18:17 ☐

- **takes place behind the person's back** – This is little more than gossip or slander – Ephesians 4:31. Everybody involved should be present to speak the truth in love to one another, and be given the opportunity to explain and account for the situation or behaviour.

Ephesians 4:31 ☐

- **is made according to human standards** – Much judgement is made on the basis of human understanding and worldly standards. The word of God and the attitudes of the kingdom are the only standard by which we can judge. John 7:24 shows that we are not to judge by the appearance but by God's righteousness.

John 7:24 ☐

- **is made about people's motives** – Only God sees and knows the inner being – the heart – of people. We rarely know our own motives, so we are extremely unlikely ever to assess correctly the motives of others – 1 Samuel 16:7 & 1 Corinthians 4:4.

1 Samuel 16:7 ☐

1 Corinthians 4:4 ☐

- **is done in an air of finality** – We must always be cautious in our judgements. Matthew 13:24–30 shows that final judgement is reserved for the king. We may be wrong, and we must articulate this possibility – as Paul does in 1 Corinthians 13:9. We must show that we are willing to change our opinion. We can never condemn another person 'out of hand' or make any final pronouncement – 1 Corinthians 4:5.

Matthew 13:24–30 ☐

1 Corinthians 13:9 ☐

4:5 ☐

- **is made without any deference to God as the Judge** – We are all called to make some judgements in different circumstances, but it is never our role 'to play God'. He alone is the Judge – James 4:12. We begin to try to usurp God's exclusive role whenever we seek some sort of revenge or try to pay back those who have wronged us – Romans 12:19 & 1 Corinthians 4:5.

James 4:12 ☐

Romans 12:19 ☐

1 Corinthians 4:5 ☐

Matthew 7:1–6 ☐

In Matthew 7:1–6, Jesus offers three compelling reasons why disciples should not judge.

1.   So that we are not judged

Matthew 7:1 states, 'Judge not, that you be not judged'. The main reason why we do not judge others is that we do not want to be judged ourselves by the king. 1 John 2:28 encourages us not to be ashamed

1 John 2:28 ☐

when we see God face to face. We need to live carefully now if we do not want to be ashamed then. If we judge others now, we will ourselves be judged then.

The New Testament describes three judgements:

- The final, basic judgement which determines our standing before God and separates believers and unbelievers, sheep from goats, those who are going to hell from those who are going to heaven.

- The on-going judgement, pruning, chastening of believers described in 1 Corinthians 5:1–8; 11:27–32.

- The judgement of rewards for believers when God allocates the inheritance and rewards which we have noted throughout our study of the kingdom. For example, 1 Corinthians 3:8; 2 Corinthians 5:9–11; Galatians 6:5 & 2 Timothy 1:16–18.

1 Corinthians
 5:1–8 ☐
 11:27–32 ☐

1 Corinthians 3:8 ☐

2 Corinthians
 5:9–11 ☐

Galatians 6:5 ☐

2 Timothy
 1:16–18 ☐

Matthew 7:1 ☐

In Matthew 7:1, Jesus is referring to the third type of judgement. When we judge others we affect our own judgement on the day when God distributes rewards and allocates the kingdom inheritance.

Disciples who judge others will not lose their salvation, but they are clearly going to lose something.

2. So that we do not set the standard of our own judgement

Matthew 7:2 ☐

Jesus' second reason for not judging is given in Matthew 7:2. When disciples judge others they not only produce a judgement on themselves, they also set the standard that God will use to judge them.

If we are quick and eager to scrutinise others and condemn them, we cannot complain when God does exactly the same to us.

3. Because we incapable of judging

Matthew 7:3–5 ☐

In Matthew 7:3–5, Jesus uses sarcasm and irony to explain that we must not judge others because we simply cannot do it properly.

He points out that, if we were really concerned with righteousness and truth, we would deal with ourselves first – we would be even more critical of ourselves than we are of others.

He says that our condition makes us incapable of helping others. The plank in our eye makes it impossible for us to remove the speck in another's. We cannot help others remove a small fault when we are blinded by an enormous plank.

He names us as hypocrites. We are not really concerned with helping the person, we are much more interested in condemning them. We pretend that we are distressed to find a small blemish, but deep inside we are delighted to point it out. According to Jesus, if we really want to help others, we will deal with our own shortcomings first.

When we truly see ourselves, we will never judge anyone else in the wrong way. The best way of ensuring that we do not have this wrong critical spirit is to make sure that we are filled with the beautiful kingdom attitudes – to be truly poor in spirit, to mourn for our poverty, to be meek and so on.

DO DISTINGUISH

In Matthew 7:1–5, Jesus instructs his disciples not to condemn other people. However he immediately goes on to show, in Matthew 7:6, that disciples must distinguish between those who are dogs and those who are not – and he points out that disciples must treat the two groups of people differently.

We must resist the temptation to be critical and to be quick to condemn people. Yet we must also recognise the New Testament instructions to 'prove all things' and 'test the spirits' – 1 Thessalonians 5:21 & 1 John 4:1–3.

1 Thessalonians 5:21 ☐

1 John 4:1–3 ☐

Jesus' words are very strong: 'Do not give what is holy to the dogs; nor cast your pearls before swine, lest they trample them under their feet, and turn and tear you in pieces.'

Just as Jesus words about judgement did not literally mean that we are never to exercise any judgement, so these words cannot mean that we are never to witness to unbelievers – for Jesus preached to them and sent the disciples to preach to them. Instead these words stress the importance of distinguishing between people and between groups of people.

The Gospels record how Jesus dealt differently with each person he met. He had one attitude towards the Pharisees and another to the ordinary people. He spoke to Pilate but was silent before Herod. At the beginning of John's gospel, he conversed with Nathaniel, Nicodemus and a Samaritan women: the truth he spoke was always the same, but he dealt with these three people in different ways.

There are five principles which we can learn from this verse.

1.   We must learn to distinguish between people

We must recognise the uniqueness of each individual person and their great value to God. We should not be mechanical in the way we relate to people, but must appreciate how we can best help each person.

If we are more concerned with what we are trying to say than the person we are trying to help, we are not filled with a Christ-like attitude.

We must also recognise that many people are fundamentally opposed to the kingdom – even though they may not realise it – and that we may need to relate to them as Christ related to the scribes and Pharisees. Many believers think that we are all called to be nice to everybody, but Matthew 23 shows that this is not so.

Matthew 23:1–36 ☐

2.   We must learn how to treat each person

We need to learn what is the appropriate help or word for each person in each situation. Following Jesus' progression, we can see that once we have removed the plank from our own eye we will be eager to help the person with a piece of dust in their eye.

We will need to learn which eye is fine and needs no attention, and which one needs gentle help. It takes tremendous care and sensitivity to remove a small speck of dust from someone's eye – we need a light touch with people, not a ham-fisted approach!

In the Gospels, we can see how Jesus treated everyone specially – and we must do the same. This means living under the personal, direct rule of God. We need to listen to his voice and not rely on our own experience. We must follow his instructions.

3.   We must learn to be careful how we treat people

Throughout the Sermon on the Mount, Jesus takes pains to point out the inevitable persecution which awaits all those who truly follow him. But in 7:6 he shows that some disciples can be needlessly torn to pieces.

This verse shows that, with care and sensitivity, we can prevent God's word from being trampled upon and ourselves from being turned on and ripped apart.

Sometimes we will be persecuted for righteousness' sake. But sometimes we will be torn to pieces because we have foolishly cast our pearls before pigs.

Jesus does not tell us to ignore the pigs or to let them starve. He merely points out the stupidity of giving them anything other than pig-food. If we know what a person is like, there is no virtue in treating them in a way which will infuriate them.

4.   We must learn to handle 'pearls' properly

When Jesus refers to pearls he is clearly referring to the message of the kingdom. In Matthew 13:44–46, Jesus likens the kingdom both to a pearl and to hidden treasure. The news about the personal rule of God is good news, but it does not appear as good news to some people. To them it is worthless, irrelevant, ridiculous.

Matthew 13:44–46 ☐

The Sermon on the Mount was Jesus' particular message to his personal disciples – it was not his words for the scribes and Pharisees, or for curious sinners. So we need to take care that we do not expect or try to impose kingdom standards upon 'pigs' and 'dogs', or that we present inappropriate truths when we are witnessing to them.

5.   We must learn to admit that some people are 'pigs'

If Jesus had not used the expression 'dogs' and 'swine', we would flinch from this truth. Yet we must face the fact that sin and darkness makes some men and women deeply antagonistic to the truth.

Titus 3:3–7 describes the effect of sin on people. It turns them into the enemies of God. Some people are so enslaved by sin, so polluted

Titus 3:3–7 ☐

and twisted by its deceptions, that they really are the spiritual equivalents of pigs and dogs. When we grasp this truth, we should be filled with compassion and sorrow. A pig cannot help acting like a pig. It cannot be reformed or cajoled into godly behaviour. It needs to be transformed by the Holy Spirit of God.

The gift of discernment

As in every area of discipleship, we need the help of the Holy Spirit if we are to distinguish correctly between different people and identify those who are 'pigs'. The spiritual gift of 'discernment' – mentioned in 1 Corinthians 12:10 – is given by the Spirit, in part, to enable us distinguish between good and evil and identify those who will turn on us and tear us to bits.

The Greek word for discernment is *diakrisis*, and this means 'thorough judging' or 'thorough separating'. It is used in Matthew 16:3; 1 Corinthians 6:5; 11:29–31; 12:10 & 14:29. The gift of discernment is a spiritual understanding which is given by God and operates in the same way as other spiritual gifts.

This shows that we need to rely on God if we are to distinguish correctly. We should not judge people on the basis of our own understanding, experience and insight, rather we assess them by depending on the insight which is given to us by God through his Spirit.

FORGIVENESS

Although Jesus does not mention forgiveness at this point in the Sermon on the Mount, it is helpful to see how we should deal with the hurt we feel when we are 'torn to pieces' by people.

Jesus teaches his disciples about forgiveness in Matthew 6:14–15. He urges them to forgive people, and states that the way they forgive others will be the way that God forgives them.

As in Matthew 7:2, Jesus is looking forward to the 'judgement of rewards'. The forgiveness he refers to is not the fundamental forgiveness of sins which determines eternal destiny, rather it is a facet of

Margin references:

1 Corinthians 12:10 ☐

Matthew 16:3 ☐

1 Corinthians 6:5 ☐
11:29–31 ☐
12:10 ☐
14:29 ☐

Matthew 6:14–15 ☐

Matthew 7:2 ☐

the distribution of rewards and inheritances to disciples which he speaks about throughout the sermon.

Jesus urged his disciples to be characterised by forgiveness in Matthew 18:21–35; and he showed them how this worked in practice by forgiving those who were literally tearing him to pieces – Luke 23:33–34.

Matthew 18:21–35 ☐
Luke 23:33–34 ☐

When people hurt us by their words or deeds, we are to forgive them. Five kingdom principles that we have already noted also apply here.

- *God is the Judge* – only he knows the real truth of what happened.

- *We have done worse ourselves* – only those without sin can throw stones.

- *They may not know what they are doing* – they may be slaves to sin.

- *We hurt ourselves* – we lose our rewards and increase our judgement by not forgiving others.

- *We are pleasing the enemy* – he wants to keep people apart.

In forgiving others, the first step is acknowledging that we have been sinned against and have been hurt as a result. Many people find it hard to admit that they are experiencing hurt feelings, but there is nothing wrong in being hurt. In fact, we can only extend forgiveness to other people when we are willing to accept that we have been wronged and hurt.

The second step is responding to the hurt in a way which honours God. We can read about this in Matthew 5:44–48; Romans 12:17–21 & 1 Peter 2:21–23. We are not called to retaliate but to offer the gift of forgiveness – which should be reinforced and followed through by specific acts of love.

Matthew 5:44–48 ☐
Romans 12:17–21 ☐
1 Peter 2:21–23 ☐

The final step is asking God to comfort us, to heal our hurts, to release us from resentment and bitterness, and to bless the person we have forgiven. 2 Corinthians 1:3–7 shows how God comforts his disciples when they are hurting.

2 Corinthians 1:3–7 ☐

PART NINE

kingdom reality

We now come to the final section of the Sermon on the Mount. In Matthew 7:7–29, Jesus sets out the realities of the kingdom and offers his disciples a series of concluding principles which are meant to help them to live in the kingdom at all times.

Matthew 7:7–29 ☐

KEEP ON SEEKING GOD

The disciples had sat listening to Jesus teach about the kingdom, and had heard him announce the standards he expected them to live by.

They had begun to realise just how different they were meant to be from the world. They had started to appreciate that they were supposed to think and to live like him. Their righteousness, their 'right being', should exceed even that of the Pharisees. They were meant to be perfect as God was perfect. Every area of their lives had to be reshaped into the nature and attitude of God. Everything they thought, everything they did, everything they were, was under the close scrutiny of the all-seeing Father. How on earth was it all going to possible?

It is easy to imagine them sitting on the mountain-side, soaking up Jesus' words, being inspired by the wonderful images he was presenting, and then suddenly realising that every word he was saying was aimed at them personally.

These principles, these impossibly high standards, were his words for each of their lives. He really expected them to live like this. He genuinely believed that their individual lives could match his words.

Matthew 7:7–29 ☐   Matthew 7:7–29 form Jesus' answer to the 'How can this be?' which must have been written across the face of every listening disciple.

As we have read Jesus' words about the kingdom, and have allowed our own lives to be scrutinised by his teaching, we must surely also have been convinced of our need for change. Most of us have probably been muttering, 'But how?' at every other verse, right through the sermon.

Matthew 7:7–27 is Jesus' answer to his first century disciples – and to us – and it begins with, 'Ask, and it will be given to you; seek, and you will find; knock and it will be opened to you.'

Jesus is telling his disciples that there is no need to despair. All we have to do is throw ourselves on the king for his enabling – to ask, to seek and to knock for his transforming provision.

Keep on asking – with persistence

We are not to ask this once, and then remain silent. Some people suggest that this sort of approach signifies faith, but we know that faith really means depending on Jesus and acting on his words.

Matthew 7:7 ☐   The Greek words used in Matthew 7:7 show that Jesus does not tell us to ask once, but to keep on asking, to keep on knocking, to keep on seeking. We can see this even more clearly in the parable which

Luke 11:5–13 ☐   illustrates these words in Luke 11:5–13.

In this instance, faith – relying on Jesus' words – means persisting to ask, seek and knock until we are personally living with all the attitudes and standards of God's kingdom.

This means that there is bound to be some spiritual discontentment within ourselves. The New Testament always encourages us to 'be content' with our material and social circumstances, but it challenges us to be discontented with our spiritual progress.

Passages like Colossians 3:1–2 & Philippians 3:12–14 urge us to 'press on', to 'keep going', to be so hungry for God and his way of living that we are continually seeking him both to transform us and to provide the strength we need to deal with sinful habits and attitudes.

At times, we will so long to be filled with the beautiful attitudes of Christ – and to live by his standards – that we will have the sort of spiritual desire to seek God we read about in Psalm 63:1. But, sometimes, our asking and seeking will be motivated more by the spiritually disciplined submission described in Hosea 10:12.

Colossians 3:1–2 ☐

Philippians 3:12–14 ☐

Psalm 63:1 ☐

Hosea 10:12 ☐

Keep on asking – believing the promise

Jesus repeats his promise, that our asking will be successful, six times in two verses – 7–8. We must remember that these are not general promises about prayer; rather, these promises specifically relate to kingdom attributes, character and standards.

- 'it will be given you'

- 'you will find'

- 'it will be opened to you'

- 'everyone who asks receives'

- 'he who seeks finds'

- 'it will be opened'

Up until this point in the sermon, Jesus has made *seventeen* promises of reward and *eleven* promises of judgement. The whole sermon pleads with believers to be sensible and to look away from the world and forward to the great day when God will reward believers according to the degree that they have pleased him.

The crescendo of promises in 7:7–8 underlines how eager God is to reward us, how keen he is to make it possible for us to please him. But, remember, he never imposes his rule on anyone – we must submit voluntarily.

Keep on asking – remembering the Father

We have seen that Jesus uses irony to emphasise several points in the sermon. He does this again in verses 9–11 to remind his disciples that living in the kingdom in the world centres upon their relationship with a good, generous, merciful heavenly Father.

Between 5:1 and 7:6, Jesus refers the disciples *fourteen* times to 'your Father'. He relentlessly drives home the point that God is watching them, is watching over them and is waiting to reward them.

Luke 11:11–13 ☐

Here, in 7:9–11, Jesus states that their Father is far better than the best human father, and that he will give good gifts to those who ask him. In Luke 11:11–13, the good gifts are seen to be the Holy Spirit.

Jesus is not promising that God will answer our prayers for earthly treasure and a comfortable life. Instead he is promising that God will give us everything we need to live the kingdom life in the world – and he is showing that the Spirit is exactly what we need. Jesus did not teach the sermon for us to comment about it, but for us to carry it out – and it is the Spirit who helps us to do this. Without his help, it is impossible for us to please God and live under his rule.

The *Sword of the Spirit* book *'Knowing the Spirit'* presents a full biblical picture of all that God wants to do in and through us by his Holy Spirit, and shows how our partnership with the Spirit works in practice.

REMEMBER THE ROYAL RULE

Matthew 7:12 ☐

Jesus' second concluding principle appears in Matthew 7:12 and is his summary of the whole sermon. Here, he reduces everything he has taught into one simple phrase which shows what living under the rule of God means in practice. 'Therefore, whatever you want men to do to you, do also to them, for this is the Law and the Prophets.'

Although Jesus does not say so, he is taking us behind the details of the Law to see the principle behind it. The real spirit of the Law is that we are to love our neighbour as ourselves – this command first appears in Leviticus 19:18, and is then returned to seven times in Matthew 19:19; 22:34–40; Mark 12:28–34; Luke 10:25–37; Romans 13:8–10; Galatians 5:14 & James 2:8–13.

Leviticus 19:18 ☐

Matthew 19:19 ☐
22:34–40 ☐

Mark 12:28–34 ☐

Luke 10:25–37 ☐

Romans 13:8–10 ☐

Galatians 5:14 ☐

James 2:8–13 ☐

The principle behind the Law insists that we are to be interested in our neighbours, that we should love them and want to help them, that we should be concerned for their well-being and happiness – even as we desire our own well-being. We are to recognise that our neighbours are people just like us – with similar feelings and failings – and we should treat them as we would like them to treat us.

Of course, this is the one thing that we find difficult. We do not do this and we do not want to do it – because we love our 'self' and are thinking about our 'self' and our desires. God always challenges this.

The kingdom deals with love of 'self' by asking us to seek God first – to put him before 'self'. The demands of his kingdom humble us and help us to focus on him and appreciate our own poverty of spirit. The demands also enable us to see others more accurately – not as people who are out to hurt us, but as fellow sinners who are crippled by sin and enslaved to *mammon*.

When we go on seeking God – and finally realise that he is a good Father who treats us with mercy and grace – we are bound to become motivated to treat others with a similar mercy and graciousness. We start seeing them as God sees us, and so begin to love them as we love ourselves.

ENTER THROUGH THE NARROW GATE

Jesus' third concluding principle, in Matthew 7:13–14, is not a summary of what has already been said. The content of the sermon has been completed, now Jesus is reminding his disciples about its urgency and is encouraging them to apply it in their everyday lives.

Matthew 7:13–14 ☐

We must grasp that these are not verses about becoming a Christian – they are verses which were spoken to disciples who were already following Jesus and who had listened to his words about the kingdom.

The disciples were being urged to appreciate that the kingdom life was not a topic for discussion, it was something to be lived. Jesus' words required an urgent response from them and some immediate action.

The disciples who were listening to Jesus had to decide whether they were going to walk home from the mountain and start living the kingdom life or carry on with their old way of following Jesus.

In these verses, Jesus presents a choice between a narrow gate, followed by a difficult path, which leads to life, and a wide gate, followed by an easy path, that leads to inevitable destruction.

A stadium turnstile or a rural kissing-gate would be the best modern parallels of Jesus' narrow gate. As we think of these pictures, we can see that they have a series of implications. None of them are new – they have all featured throughout the sermon.

- **we cannot take anything with us** – the gate is too narrow for any baggage, we must leave everything behind – the world, the way of the world, 'self', *mammon*, and so on

- **we must pass through on our own** – it is a personal, individual response

- **we must be ready for difficulties** – persecution, isolation, hardships and suffering are all guaranteed

- **we will be different** – we will stand out from the crowd, we will be in a minority, we will be unusual and exceptional, we will be mocked for taking a difficult path

- **we must look to the future** – we are heading for life, this is the fact which keeps us going – the other path may be easier at the moment, but it is heading for certain destruction

We have already noted that judgement is the great theme of chapter seven. From verse 13 to the end of the chapter, Jesus repeatedly refers to the issue of judgement to stress the fact that kingdom issues are matters of life and death. For example, he speaks about 'destruction' – verse 13, 'life' – verse 14; 'the fire' – verse 19; and 'that day' – verse 22.

It is eternally important we make sure that we are on his narrow way, that we make all the hard choices he puts before us, and that we are ready to 'count the cost' of the kingdom because of the glories which are before us.

Matthew 7:13 ☐
7:14 ☐
7:19 ☐
7:22 ☐

WATCH OUT FOR FALSE PROPHETS

Jesus' fourth concluding principle – in verses 15–20 – warns disciples contemplating the narrow path to beware of false prophets and shows them that kingdom living is meant to bear good fruit.

Matthew 7:15–20 ☐

We know that kingdom living means being ruled by God. We do not depend on a code or system, we rely on God and his word. In placing his warning about false prophets at this point in the sermon, Jesus makes it plain that there will be those who claim to know and speak God's word who will tempt us away from the narrow path.

False prophets claim to bring the word of God, but God has not sent them – we see this in Jeremiah 23:9–40. Jesus is not speaking about people who are plainly false – about teachers who are obvious heretics or living blatantly sinful lives. He is referring to those who look like sheep – who seem harmless – but underneath are ravenous wolves.

Jeremiah
    23:9–40 ☐

In the Old Testament, Deuteronomy 13:1–5; 18:21–22; Jeremiah 23:9–40 & Ezekiel 12:21 – 14:11 provide five tests for false prophets:

Deuteronomy
    13:1–5 ☐
    18:21–22 ☐

Ezekiel 12:21–
    14:11 ☐

- the failure of their predictive prophecies (although the corollary is not necessarily true: fulfilment is not a proof of genuineness)

- they call people after other gods

- their lifestyles are immoral

- they do not check immorality in others

- they call for peace without any regard to the moral and spiritual conditions required for peace

Jesus shows that we must not judge people by their superficial appearance, but by the effect, the fruit of the person's ministry and life. It is not clear whether Jesus' reference to 'fruit' means the teaching, the personal lifestyle, or the results of a prophet – he probably means all three. The principles found in Acts 10:43 and Revelation 19:10 are crucial. All true prophets point to Jesus – to his life, to his standards and to his work.

Acts 10:43 ☐

Revelation 19:10 ☐

Anybody who claims to know or to speak the word of God is false if they are calling disciples away from the difficult, narrow way; if they are not living the narrow kingdom life for themselves; and if those who listen to them do not progress along the narrow path to life.

We must 'beware' for the enemy will do anything possible to distract disciples from God and to lead us away from the king's narrow, difficult footpath onto his smooth and easy motorway.

Jesus' use of the fruit picture reminds us again that kingdom thinking is meant to make a difference to the way we live and to the people around us. Our change in thinking should lead to changed behaviour. Our attitudes should become our actions. The salt and light should do all the things that we noted. Verse 19 makes it plain that if God's rule in our lives does not bear good fruit, we will experience his judgement.

THE TRUE TEST

Matthew 7:21–23 ☐

The fifth principle – verses 21–23 – teaches that the true test of kingdom living is not what we say, nor the gifts we exercise, but doing the will of the Father.

Again, it is vital we never forget that Jesus is talking to disciples throughout the sermon – these verses are not about becoming a Christian, they are about living the Christian life. We must keep on remembering that the judgement Jesus refers to throughout the sermon is not the basic judgement which divides believers from unbelievers and consigns people to heaven or hell; it is the judgement of rewards which only believers will face.

Jesus is not saying that people who are disciples – who know Jesus as Lord, and have shared his authority and passed on his word – will be banished to hell. Instead, he is saying that there will be many surprises on 'the day' when rewards and inheritances are distributed. There will be disciples who have apparently done great deeds for the kingdom who will be sent away from the king unrewarded. This is a persistent theme of Jesus in all his teaching about the kingdom.

In the end, pleasing God comes down to doing the will of the Father. The rule of God means submitting to the king in every area and detail of living. Heavenly rewards are earned by obeying the words of Jesus. Judgement comes from presuming to do our own will or refusing to do God's will. There is no other test of faith.

PUTTING IT ALL INTO PRACTICE

The sermon ends with a story. Jesus has finished his detailed instruction and laid down his great principles; now he is applying his truth. He has confronted his disciples with two possibilities – the narrow or the broad way – and has shown them how to avoid the dangers which will face them. Here, in verses 24–27, he tells them a story to illustrate everything he has said.

Matthew 7:24–27 ☐

There were two men and two houses. Both men wanted exactly the same thing – a house in which they could live with their families. They built houses which were close to each other and very similar. In fact, superficially, the two houses looked exactly the same. Jesus seems to suggest that the men must have had much in common.

However, in Luke 6:46–51 we can see that there are real differences between them. The foolish man is impatient: he wants his house now – there is no time for foundations. He does not look forward to see possible consequences or bother to learn from others. Whereas the wise man wants to build well and to last. He does not take any short cuts. He is ready to learn. He thinks before he acts.

Luke 6:46–51 ☐

The houses may have looked the same, but the invisible foundations were different. Two prophets may seem harmless, but underneath they are different. Two disciples who prophesy and cast out demons may look the same but have quite different foundations.

In all these illustrations, Jesus is imploring us to be discriminating, to look beyond appearances, to see that the only thing which matters is doing the will of God.

When trouble came in the story, the foolish man's house collapsed and the wise man's house survived. Living in the kingdom does not provide us with immunity from trouble – we know that exactly the opposite is true. But living under the rule of God does provide us with the strength to endure through the hardships onto the rewards – if we have the right foundations.

Jesus uses the story to summarise everything he has taught about the kingdom. Right at the end of the sermon, he reminds us that his kingdom is supremely practical – it is about building lives which last and endure – and that God's rule promises us peace of mind in the present, strength in great trial, and wonderful assurance for the future.

Recognising Jesus' authority

The sermon is over, but Matthew 7 continues for two more verses to record the disciples' reaction. Verses 28–39 comment, 'And so it was, when Jesus had ended these sayings, that the people were astonished at his teaching, for he taught them as one having authority, and not as the scribes.'

It is easy for us to be so pre-occupied with the content of Jesus' teaching that we ignore the Teacher. At the end of the sermon, these verses re-direct our attention to him and to his unique personal authority.

If we have been paying attention, we will have seen that Jesus continually draws our attention to himself throughout the sermon. He speaks about himself and his words over twenty times during the sermon and makes it graphically clear that he himself is the only basis for what he is saying. We can see this in 5:11, 17, 18, 20, 22, 26, 28, 32, 34, 39, 44; 6:2, 5, 16, 25, 29; 7:21, 22, 23, 24 & 26.

Quite simply, our personal recognition of Jesus' authority is measured by the extent to which we start to seek God and begin to depend entirely on his rule. If we genuinely seek him and his right way of being first – before everything else in our lives – we will be building on the best foundation for life and will be heading for wonderful heavenly rewards.

As Jesus has made so transparently clear, nothing else makes sense for disciples. God's way may be difficult, but it does lead to the life for which we long. Only disciples who are foolish do not travel along the narrow path of the kingdom. Wise disciples make sure that they are ruled by God and that they depend entirely on his word and his Spirit.

ACTIVITIES for individuals and small groups

the kingdom

The kingdom of God – or the kingdom of heaven – is the main theme of Jesus' teaching. He teaches more about this than any other topic. Matthew's gospel calls it 'the kingdom of heaven', whereas Mark and Luke use 'the kingdom of God'.

Does the phrase 'the kingdom of God' describe the people ruled by God or the ruling activity of God? Why is this important?

....

....

What do these passages teach about 'the kingdom'? Psalm 22:28; 103:19; 145:8–13; Daniel 4:25; Matthew 6:10 & Luke 11:2.

....

....

....

What does John the Baptist teach about the kingdom in Matthew 3:1–12 and Luke 3:7–20?

....

....

....

THE PRESENT KINGDOM

Jesus began his ministry by announcing in Mark 1:14–15 that the time had come and the kingdom of God was at hand. In Matthew 12:28 and Luke 11:20, he repeats his claim that the kingdom has come and evidences this by casting out demons.

What does Jesus' authority over evil spirits show about the kingdom?

....

....

....

The kingdom came in and with Jesus. As the Messiah, Jesus is central to everything the Gospels announce about the kingdom, and the kingdom is central to everything he teaches.

What do these passages teach about Jesus and the kingdom that came in and with him?

Matthew 3:16–17 ....

Matthew 5:17 ....

Matthew 7:23 ....

Matthew 17:5 ....

Matthew 21:27 ....

Matthew 25:41 ....

Mark 1:38 ....

Mark 10:45 ....

Luke 4:21 ....

Luke 19:10 ....

THE FUTURE KINGDOM

As well as teaching that the kingdom had come, Jesus also taught that elements of the kingdom were still to come.

What do these passages teach about the coming kingdom?

Matthew 5:1–10 ....

Matthew 6:10 ....

Matthew 7:21–22 ....

Matthew 8:11 ....

Matthew 13:42–43 ....

Matthew 16:27–28 ....

Matthew 20:21 ....

Matthew 26:29 ....

Mark 9:1 ....

Mark 10:37 ....

Mark 14:25 ....

Luke 13:28–29 ....

Luke 22:18 ....

Do you focus more on the present or the future elements of the kingdom? How can you embrace both elements more fully?

....

....

....

ASPECTS OF THE KINGDOM

If we are to understand the kingdom rightly, we must appreciate that: [1] it belongs to God; [2] it is dynamic and powerful; [3] it is established by Jesus; [4] it is for salvation.

The coming of the kingdom shows God's kingly activity in reaching out to save and bless people of every nation and generation – we see this evidenced in his miracles.

What is the most prominent miracle in the proclamation of the kingdom?

....

....

THE MYSTERY OF THE KINGDOM

Much of Jesus' teaching about the kingdom was given as parables. Matthew 13:1–52; Mark 4:10–12 & Luke 8:9–10 explain why he taught in this way.

Why did Jesus use parables to teach about the kingdom?

....

....

....

....

What are the implications of this for your evangelism?

....

....

....

What principles can we learn about the kingdom in the Matthew 13, 21, 22 & 25 parables?

....

....

....

....

....

....

....

THE KINGDOM IN THE NEW TESTAMENT

The term 'the kingdom' does not often appear outside the first three gospels. However, the concepts of the personal rule of God and freedom from the Mosaic Law run through the New Testament. Phrases like 'the Lordship of Christ' are used instead of 'the kingdom', but they merely express the same truth in different words.

What do these passages teach about the kingdom?

John 3:1–21 ....

John 18:33–38 ....

Acts 19:8; 20:24–25 & 28:23, 31 ....

Romans 14:17 ....

1 Thessalonians 2:12 ....

1 Corinthians 15:50 ....

Hebrews 12:28 ....

James 2:5 ....

Revelation 1:9; 11:15; 12:10 ....

the call of the kingdom

Mark 1:14–15; Matthew 3:1 & 4:17 show that the coming of the kingdom was not an event which merely had to be announced, its coming was a challenge to which people had to respond.

THE CALL TO REPENT

What does biblical repentance mean?

....

....

How does Romans 12:2 relate to the idea of repentance?

....

....

....

What has repentance meant – specifically – for you?

....

....

....

What do these verses teach about repentance?

Luke 24:47 ....

Luke 13:3–5 ....

Luke 5:32 ....

Luke 15:7, 70 ....

Acts 2:38 ....

Acts 17:30 ....

Acts 20:21 ....

Acts 5:31; 11:18 ....

THE CALL TO BELIEVE

When we grasp that 'to repent' means 'to change your mind', it becomes clear why 'believe' is the second call. Any change of mind must involve believing new things.

For many people, 'believing' is an intellectual act. But 'belief' in the New Testament involves action; it is the application of repentance.

What is involved in believing?

....

....

What is the link between faith and believing?

....

....

To believe in the gospel means to believe in Jesus himself. The people listening to Jesus were expected to commit themselves to all that Jesus stood for – for his whole mission.

John 20:30–31 shows that the whole purpose of the gospel is that we might 'believe'. This gospel is packed with over one hundred statements about believing.

What do these verses teach about believing? John 1:12; 2:11; 3:16–17; 4:50; 8:30; 10:38; 12:11; 14:1, 10.

....

....

....

....

....

How is belief expressed in these verses? John 5:24; 6:40; 6:45; 8:43, 47; 12:45, 47; 14:7, 9; 17:23 & 18:37.

....

....

....

....

Personal belief in Jesus was the distinguishing mark of Christians. They not only had to change their minds about him, they also had to trust, believe, depend on Christ himself before they could appropriate what he had done for them through his death and resurrection.

How did your belief in Jesus begin, and how has it developed?

....
....
....
....

How does your belief in Jesus affect the way you live?

....
....
....
....

THE CALL TO DISCIPLESHIP

Matthew 4:17–22 & Mark 1:15–20 show how Jesus moved on from announcing the kingdom's arrival, through calling people to repent and believe in the gospel, to call specific people personally to follow him. When we start to believe in Jesus, we find that he calls us to demonstrate our belief by following him – by becoming a disciple.

What does the word 'disciple' mean?

....
....

In Matthew 11:28–30, Jesus calls us to learn from him personally – this is true discipleship. Just as he does not call us to follow a set of ideas or rules but to follow him, so he does not call us to learn from the Law or from a book but rather to learn from him himself.

How do you learn from Jesus?

....
....

How did people respond to Jesus' call in these passages?

Matthew 4:18–22 ....

Matthew 9:9 ....

Matthew 19:21 ....

Luke 9:59 ....

John 1:43 ....

How, specifically, have you been challenged to follow Jesus in the last month?

....

....

....

What do these verse teach about discipleship? Matthew 6:33; Luke 12:31–34; Matthew 16:13–33; Luke 9:23.

....

....

....

What has 'carrying a cross' and 'giving up everything' meant for you?

....

....

....

THE CALL TO BE CHRIST-LIKE

How are we called to love?

....

....

How does being a disciple affect the way that you give?

....

....

How does Mark 10:45 relate to Daniel 7:13–14?

....

....

How are you applying Philippians 2:5–11 in your life?

....

....

....

What are the works referred to in John 14:12?

....

....

THE CALL TO INHERIT THE KINGDOM

Our Christ-like loving, giving, serving, working and going is not unrewarded. Jesus makes it plain that there are an ample inheritance and many rewards before us.

What will we inherit?

....

....

....

What will qualify us to inherit?

....

....

When will we receive our inheritance and rewards?

....

....

What will reduce our rewards and inheritance?

....

....

the attitudes of the kingdom

The Sermon on the Mount is Jesus' teaching for his disciples. It describes God's radical lifestyle for people who have obeyed his 'follow me' and have begun to live under God's rule. It sets out the attitudes which characterise true disciples. The introduction to the sermon, 5:3–12, is usually called 'the beatitudes', and this is a list of eight basic attitudes which Jesus develops throughout the rest of his sermon.

The beatitudes or 'beautiful attitudes' give a general character description of those disciples who are living 'in the kingdom'. If we live fully under the personal rule of God, we can expect to be characterised by these attitudes.

POOR IN SPIRIT

What does it mean to be poor in spirit?

....

....

What do these verses teach about poverty of spirit?

Ephesians 2:1–10 ....

Matthew 23:25–28 ....

Isaiah 6:5 ....

Luke 5:8 ....

What do unbelievers think about poverty of spirit?

....

....

....

How do you display your poverty of spirit?

....

....

....

....

How was Jesus poor in spirit?

....

....

MOURNING

What should we mourn about?

Our sinful nature, jealousy envy, work, forgive and
forget.

....

What did Jesus mourn about?

Jerusalem, friends who argued

....

How does God reward those who mourn?

Comfort.

....

MEEKNESS

What do these verses teach about meekness?

Philippians 4:5 ....

Galatians 6:1 ....

Matthew 11:28–30   Find rest ....

Isaiah 50:4–5 ....

1 Corinthians 13:5 ....

Romans 12:17–21 ....

1 Peter 2:23 ....

How did Jesus show meekness?

Being a servant, washed there feet. Following the father went to
calvary to be crucified without saying a word.

When do you find it difficult to be meek?

w) critisism.   m) Previously disadvantage   mat : Previously Disad.
kee) Short changed not able to express   sean. Angry.
mandy : Crit / people who talk.

How will we inherit the earth?

w) Seed to sow.   m) What the Lord wants mat :
kee) Needs of others   sean : Work in Progress. PATIENCE.
mat : Patience.   mandy : People 1st.

HUNGRY FOR RIGHTEOUSNESS

The first four attitudes underline the spiritual bankruptcy and inadequacy felt by disciples. They are poor in spirit, they mourn, they are meek before God and other people, they are empty and want to be filled.

How is Jeremiah 2:13 a picture of modern society?

Worshiping other GODS.

What is righteousness?

Seek he 1st   Conforming to GODS will.

Why is it better to want to be righteous than to want to be happy?

To be in the will of GOD

How desperate are you to think and live like Jesus?

Personal.

What difference does this spiritual hunger make to your life?

Question decisions, Gives guidance.

MERCIFUL

Why do we all need mercy?

....

....

How can we show mercy to others?

....

....

PURE IN HEART

What do we learn from the order of the attitudes?

....

....

Why is Jesus more concerned with internal than external matters?

....

....

What is purity of heart?

....

....

In what way is your heart not pure?

....

....

What does it mean to see God?

....

....

PEACEMAKERS

The attitudes show that people who are filled with God have three positive characteristics –
mercy, purity and peacemaking. These are key ingredients in disciples who are ruled by God.

How are you a peacemaker?

....

....

How was Jesus a peacemaker?

....

....

Which parts of the Sermon on the Mount illustrate peacemaking?

....

....

....

PERSECUTED

Today, we feel sorry for those who are persecuted. We try to support them. We campaign for them. We sometimes admire them; but we do not envy them or think that they are fortunate. Jesus does – if they are persecuted for righteousness' sake.

What is meant by 'righteousness' sake'?

....

....

Why does the world persecute disciples who are filled with these attitudes?

....

....

What does this teach about effective evangelism?

....

....

....

Why is the reward for the eighth attitude the same as the one for the first?

....

....

the world and the kingdom

As disciples who have entered the kingdom, we are caught in the tension between the 'world' and the 'kingdom', for we have to live in both at the same time. The first section of the Sermon on the Mount after the beatitudes, Matthew 5:11–16, deals with the world's reaction to the kingdom and the kingdom's response to the world.

What is meant by 'the world'?

....

....

....

THE WORLD'S OPPOSITION

How do these verses show that the world and the kingdom are opposed?

Matthew 5:11 ....

Luke 6:22 ....

John 1:10 ....

John 7:7 ....

John 12:31 ....

John 17:9, 14, 16 ....

Romans 3:16 ....

1 Corinthians 2:12 ....

Ephesians 2:12 ....

Philippians 2:15 ....

Colossians 1:13 ....

1 John 2:15–16 ....

1 John 3:1 ....

1 John 3:13 ....

1 John 4:1 ....

1 John 4:3 ....

1 John 5:19 ....

THE KINGDOM'S RESPONSE

We are called to respond to the world's opposition by enduring all things, by loving and forgiving our persecutors, and by rejoicing when we are persecuted.

What opposition have you had to face because of your faith?

....

....

How did you respond to this opposition?

....

....

How, practically, can we forgive our persecutors?

....

....

How can we rejoice in persecution?

....

....

LIVING THE KINGDOM IN THE WORLD

Jesus wants us to be deeply involved with the world and prays that God will keep us safe in the world. If we are truly to live under the rule of God we have to be in the world.

In what ways are we 'in' the world but not 'of' the world?

....

....

What does it mean to be 'salt' of the earth?

....

....

....

How do we keep our saltiness?

....

....

How do we shine as light in the world?

....

....

How do you speak out against injustice, immorality, corruption – and so on – in your family and community?

....

....

....

....

What good deeds are you doing which are causing people to glorify God?

....

....

....

....

What steps should you take to improve the message you are giving to people about the kingdom through your attitudes and actions?

....

....

....

....

....

righteousness in the kingdom

We know that, as disciples of Jesus Christ, we have been called to live under the personal rule of God – a rule which is always consistent with the unchanging nature of God.

We also know that Jesus is more concerned with our attitudes than our actions, but that he wants our attitudes to lead to actions which are consistent with his character – and with God's nature. He wants our righteousness – our right being – to exceed even that of the Pharisees.

RIGHTEOUSNESS AND THE LAW

What is the Law and the Prophets?

....

How did Jesus fulfil the Law?

....

....

....

What did Jesus' fulfilment of the Law result in?

....

....

How can our righteousness exceed the Pharisees?

....

....

....

What is the difference between Christian righteousness and living under the Law?

....

....

....

ANGER

Jesus contrasts 'You have heard' with 'but I say to you' six times. How can we understand this?

....
....
....

Why is anger viewed so strongly in the kingdom?

....
....
....

How, practically, can we take the initiative in reconciliation?

....
....
....

What does Jesus do to the Law?

....
....
....
....

SEXUAL PURITY

Why are lustful thoughts viewed so strongly in the kingdom?

....
....

What practical steps have you taken to avoid compromise and sin in this area?

....
....

MARRIAGE

How should we apply Jesus' teaching about divorce in today's society?

....

....

....

Does his teaching apply equally to believers and unbelievers?

....

....

TRUTHFULNESS

What practical difference has Jesus' teaching made to the way you speak about things?

....

....

....

What should your response be if you are asked to make an oath – for example, in court?

....

....

What do you catch yourself exaggerating about? How do Jesus' words here relate to exaggeration?

....

....

....

RIGHTS

Please re-read verses 39–42. These are among the most radical of all Jesus teaching – little is more contrary to the attitude and thinking of the modern world than these principles.

Which of these verses do you find the hardest to put into practice? Why is this?

....

....

What exceptions do you think we should make to these principles?

....

....

....

When would it be right for you to insist on your rights?

....

....

LOVE

Who are your enemies?

....

....

How, practically can you do good to them?

....

....

Which areas of your life has God spoken to you about?

....

....

....

What changes does God want you to make in your attitudes and actions?

....

....

....

spiritual life in the kingdom

In Matthew 5, Jesus outlines the character of disciples, describes how they should behave in society, and lists the standards he expects them to live by. In Matthew 6, he offers a picture of disciples living the kingdom life in the world, and emphasises that we live in the world in the presence of the all-seeing God. Verses 1–18 deal with our spiritual lives and verses 19–34 focus on our ordinary 'everyday' lives. The kingdom is not concerned with only one or two areas of our lives – God wants to rule in every aspect of our living.

PRINCIPLES OF KINGDOM SPIRITUALITY

Living in the kingdom means that our lives are constantly open and exposed before the king. Because we live in the presence of God, we can have no secrets from him and should be real in our relationship with him.

Matthew 6:1 lays down four general principles: [1] We are called to attract attention towards us so that people glorify *God*, yet we must not attract any attention towards us so that people focus on *us*. [2] We should act in such a way that our sole aim is to please God. [3] God sees all our thoughts and actions; there is nothing we can think or do which is missed by him. [4] If we do the right thing for the right reason, we will be rewarded by God.

In what ways are you tempted to attract attention to yourself by the way you worship and talk about your spiritual life?

....
....
....
....
....

How can you ensure that people glorify God more because of your life?

....
....
....
....

GIVING GOD'S WAY

In Matthew 6:2–4, Jesus is not talking about giving money, instead he is speaking about helping people in the widest possible way. This involves giving money, time, attention – any kind deeds.

How does God reward real giving?

....

....

How do you let people know what you have done?

....

....

....

What mental records do you keep of your giving and serving?

....

....

....

PRAYING GOD'S WAY

In Matthew 6:5–15, Jesus tells us to be real in our praying by [1] not showing off; [2] not having a set formula; and [3] by focusing on approaching God.

How do we show off in our praying today?

....

....

....

What set routines or formula do you have for prayer?

....

....

....

How can we use the Lord's Prayer as a pattern for our praying?

....

....

....

Using the Lord's Prayer as a pattern, write a prayer about your immediate needs.

....

....

....

....

....

....

....

....

....

....

....

FASTING GOD'S WAY

In Matthew 6:16–18, Jesus shows his disciples how to be real in their fasting. Because Jesus has fulfilled the entire Old Testament, there is now no legal reason for fasting. But this does not mean that we must not fast. Rather, it means that we do not have to fast either to be righteous or as a legalistic duty. Jesus does not condemn fasting, he merely condemns fasting with wrong motives.

What is fasting?

....

....

What are some wrong reasons for fasting?

....

....

....

What are some good reasons for fasting?

....

....

....

When and why have you fasted?

....

....

....

....

In what ways do you slip into showy forms of worship? Please give some specific examples.

....

....

....

....

How can we help each other to guard against this?

....

....

....

....

What has God said to you about the spiritual dimension of your life?

....

....

....

What are you going to do?

....

....

....

physical life in the kingdom

Matthew 6 considers two aspects of a disciple's life. Verses 1–18 deal with the spiritual dimension and verses 19–34 focus on the physical dimension. Verses 19–34 suggest that we must keep on asking, 'Who is my master?' and 'Who am I serving?' for God will tolerate no rival powers in the lives of his subjects.

Jesus deals with two problems or temptations in 19–34: [1] that we must not *serve* or love the world; and [2] that we must not *worry* about the world.

GOD OR MAMMON?

Mammon is the Aramaic word for wealth or riches, and Jesus' use of it suggests that 'wealth' is a rival to God for our affections. *Mammon* is a power which attempts to dominate and enslave us – when we should be ruled only by God.

What does money offer that God wants us to find only in him?

....

....

....

What do these verses teach us about mammon *and discipleship?*

Luke 5:27–28 ....

Luke 5:1–11 ....

Luke 18:18–23 ....

Matthew 10:7–10 ....

Luke 10:1–12 ....

How do we store up heavenly treasure?

....

....

....

We serve *mammon* not just be putting our trust in wealth and hanging on to what we have, but also by constantly thinking about material things – by seeing them in our 'mind's eye', by day-dreaming about how our life would improve if only we had this or that.

How does mammon *affect you?*

....

....

How do you resist mammon?

....

....

What does the story in 2 Kings 17:24–41 teach us?

....

....

What 'gods' are you tempted still to serve?

....

....

WORRY OR FAITH?

In Matthew 6:25–34, Jesus emphasises the pointlessness of worrying about earthly things. We may not have many possessions, but we can still be in the grip of *mammon* because we are always worrying about the physical problems of life.

He is warning us not to be distracted from a disciple's main objective with worries about the physical matters of life. He is not saying that we must *never* think about food and clothes; rather he is urging us not to allow these things to distract us from focusing on God's word.

What are the reasons that Jesus gives for not worrying?

....

....

....

....

What do you worry about most?

....

....

How can you put Jesus' words into practice?

....

....

After explaining why disciples should not worry about physical needs, Jesus offers three important conclusions: [1] be different from the pagans; [2] know that God knows; and [3] concentrate on the kingdom.

How do your home and possessions show that you are different from unbelievers?

....

....

....

What is your experience of God providing practically for you?

....

....

....

What do you treasure more than anything else? What evidence is there that this is true?

....

....

....

What do you worry about with regard to the future?

....

....

What has God said to you through these verses?

....

....

....

judgement in the kingdom

Judgement is the main theme of chapter seven. Jesus begins with a clear and simple statement, 'Judge not', which he follows with three reasons why disciples should not judge others.

DO NOT JUDGE

Jesus does mean that disciples must never express any opinions – for verses 6 & 15 would be impossible to apply if this were so. Rather he is concerned with the way that we criticise and condemn others. He is forbidding the wrong kind of judging. He is warning us against the critical attitude which condemns other people and regards them with contempt.

When are judgement and criticism wrong?

....

....

....

....

What do these verses teach about judging others?

Ephesians 4:2–5 ....

Ephesians 4:31–32 ....

Philippians 4:5 ....

James 2:1–4 ....

John 7:24 ....

1 Corinthians 4:4–5 ....

Matthew 13:24–30 ....

James 4:12 ....

Romans 12:19 ....

How should we respond to unjust criticism?

....

....

How can we avoid making judgements according to human standards?

....

....

In Matthew 7:1–6, Jesus offers three compelling reasons why disciples should not judge: [1] so that we are not judged; [2] so that we do not set the standard of our own judgement; and [3] because we incapable of judging.

What is the judgement we face?

....

....

Is Jesus' teaching that we can lose our salvation?

....

....

Who is really qualified to judge another?

....

....

Why does it seem easier to see faults in others before we see our own?

....

....

....

What are the planks in your eye?

....

....

....

When we truly see ourselves, we will never judge anyone else in the wrong way. The best way of ensuring that we do not have this wrong critical spirit is to make sure that we are filled with the beautiful kingdom attitudes – to be truly poor in spirit, to mourn for our poverty, to be meek and so on.

DO DISTINGUISH

In Matthew 7:1–5, Jesus instructs his disciples not to condemn other people. However he goes on to show, in Matthew 7:6, that disciples must distinguish between those who are 'dogs' and those who are not – and treat the two groups differently.

We must resist the temptation to be critical and to be quick to condemn people. Yet we must also recognise the New Testament instructions to 'prove all things' and 'test the spirits' – 1 Thessalonians 5:21 & 1 John 4:1–3.

These words cannot mean that we are never to witness to unbelievers – for Jesus preached to them and sent the disciples to preach to them – instead they stress the importance of distinguishing between people and between groups of people.

What are the implications of these verses for the way we evangelise?

....

....

....

....

....

What were the different ways that Jesus related to people?

....

....

....

....

There are five principles to learn from these verses: we must learn [1] to distinguish between people; [2] how to treat each person; [3] to be careful how we treat people; [4] to handle 'pearls' properly; [5] to admit that some people are 'pigs'.

Have you ever been hurt because you have tried to give a 'pearl' to a 'pig'? What did you learn from this experience?

....

....

....

How, practically, should we handle 'pearls'?

....

....

What does Titus 3:3–7 teach about the effects of sin on people?

....

....

How do we identify a 'dog' or a 'pig'?

....

....

FORGIVENESS

Jesus teaches his disciples about forgiveness in Matthew 6:14–15. He urges them to forgive people, and states that the way they forgive others will be the way that God forgives them.

What principles of the kingdom apply to forgiveness?

....

....

....

....

How, practically, do we forgive people?

....

....

Whom do you need to forgive?

....

....

Whom do you need to be forgiven by?

....

....

kingdom reality

In the final section of the Sermon, Matthew 7:7–29, Jesus sets out the realities of the kingdom and offers his disciples a series of principles to help them to live in the kingdom at all times.

KEEP ON SEEKING GOD

When we have subjected our lives to the scrutiny of Jesus' teaching, and have seen our need to change, we do not need to despair. Instead, we should throw ourselves on God for his help. Verses 7–11 show that we should keep on asking: [1] with persistence; [2] believing the promise; and [3] remembering the Father.

How does our persistence in seeking God show our faith?

....
....

What are you discontented about spiritually?

....
....

What do Jesus' promises in verses 7–8 relate to?

....
....

Why are the promises of reward emphasised so heavily in the sermon?

....
....

Why does Jesus keep on pointing us to the Father in the sermon?

....
....

What are the good things promised to us?

....
....

REMEMBER THE ROYAL RULE

Matthew 7:12 is Jesus' summary of the whole sermon. He reduces everything he has taught into one simple phrase which shows what living under the rule of God means in practice.

How does this verse sum up the whole teaching of the Sermon on the Mount?

....

....

....

What do you find hard about 'loving your neighbour as yourself'?

....

....

....

How, practically, does living in the kingdom help you to love your neighbour as yourself?

....

....

....

ENTER THROUGH THE NARROW GATE

In Matthew 7:13–14, Jesus reminds his disciples about the urgency of his words about the kingdom, and encourages them to apply them in their everyday lives.

How do Jesus' words apply to people who are not Christians?

....

....

....

How far should we try to change the laws of our society to reflect kingdom principles?

....

....

....

What is the narrow way? How is it difficult?

....

....

What have been the greatest difficulties for you on the narrow way?

....

....

What attracts you most about the broad way?

....

....

Why are you on the narrow way?

....

....

Why does Jesus stress issues of judgement so much in these verses?

....

....

WATCH OUT FOR FALSE PROPHETS

In verses 15–20, Jesus warns disciples contemplating the narrow path to beware of false prophets and shows them that kingdom living is meant to bear good fruit.

What is a false prophet?

....

....

How, practically, can we identify a false prophet?

....

....

What is the difference between a false prophet and someone who makes a mistake when prophesying?

....

....

What are the true signs of genuine prophetic ministry?

....

....

What is the significance of the 'fruit' picture?

....

....

What will happen to us if we do not bear good fruit?

....

....

THE TRUE TEST

Verses 21–23 teach that the true test of kingdom living is not what we say, nor the gifts we exercise, but doing the will of the Father.

Jesus is not saying that people who are disciples – who know Jesus as Lord, and have shared his authority and passed on his word – will be banished to hell. Instead, he is saying that there will be many surprises on 'the day' when rewards are distributed. There will be disciples who have apparently done great deeds for the kingdom who will be sent away unrewarded.

Why are our words not enough?

....

....

In what areas of your life do you struggle most with God's will?

....

....

In the end, pleasing God comes down to doing the will of the Father. The rule of God means submitting to the king in every area and detail of living. Heavenly rewards are earned by obeying the words of Jesus. Judgement comes from presuming to do our own will or refusing to do God's will. There is no other test of faith.

PUTTING IT ALL INTO PRACTICE

The Sermon on the Mount ends with a story – in verses 24–27 – which illustrates everything Jesus has said.

What are the differences between the two men?

....

....

In what way are you like the wise man and like the foolish man?

....

....

What is the point of this story?

....

....

After the sermon, Matthew 7 continues for two more verses to record the disciples' reaction. 'The people were astonished at his teaching, for he taught them as one having authority, and not as the scribes.'

How can we recognise Jesus' authority in our lives?

....

....

What changes has Jesus asked you to make in your life through these studies?

....

....

What is the most important thing you have learnt through these studies?

....

....

....

....

....